MGB
DRIVER'S HANDBOOK

MGB
TOURER AND GT

The British Motor Corporation Limited
MG Car division

ABINGDON-ON-THAMES · BERKSHIRE · ENGLAND

Telephone: Abingdon 251-2-3-4   *Telegrams:* Emgee, Abingdon

Overseas Business
BMC EXPORT SALES LIMITED
a Subsidiary of The British Motor Corporation Limited

LONGBRIDGE · BIRMINGHAM · ENGLAND

Telephone: Priory 2101   *Telex:* SPEEDILY, Birmingham 33491
Cables: SPEEDILY, Birmingham, England

Publication Part No. AKD 3900 J

THE 'MGB' GT
THE 'MGB' TOURER

FOREWORD

YOU will find in these pages an introduction to your vehicle and information essential to satisfactory use and maintenance.

A Passport to Service containing service vouchers is provided, and the regular use of the vouchers in sequence is the best safeguard against the possibility of abnormal repair bills at a later date. Replacement Passport to Service books are obtainable free of charge from Distributors or Dealers. Prevent rather than cure.

Completed voucher counterfoils are proof of regular servicing and could well enhance the value of your vehicle in the eyes of a prospective buyer.

By keeping the Passport to Service, signed by the Distributor, Dealer or vendor, in the vehicle you can quickly establish the date of purchase and provide the necessary details if adjustments are required to be carried out under warranty.

Claims for the replacement of parts under warranty must be submitted to the supplying Distributor or Dealer or, when this is not possible, to the nearest Distributor or Dealer, informing them of the vendor's name and address. Except in cases of emergency, warranty work should always be carried out by a BMC appointed Distributor or Dealer.

When Service Parts are required insist on BMC GENUINE PARTS as these are designed and tested for your vehicle and in addition have the full backing of the BMC Factory Warranty. ONLY WHEN GENUINE PARTS ARE USED CAN BMC ACCEPT RESPONSIBILITY.

**The British Motor Corporation Limited
BMC Service division**

COWLEY · OXFORD · ENGLAND

Telephone: Oxford 77777.   *Telegrams:* BMCSERV. Telex. Oxford
Telex: BMCSERV. Oxford 83145 and 83146
Overseas Cables: BMCSERV. Telex. Oxford. England

GENERAL DATA

Engine

Bore	3·16 in. (80·26 mm.)
Stroke	3·5 in. (89 mm.)
No. of cylinders	4
Capacity	1798 c.c. (109·8 cu. in.)
Compression ratio: High compression	8·8 : 1
Low compression	8·0 : 1
Firing order	1, 3, 4, 2
Valve clearance (cold)	·015 in. (·38 mm.)
Oil pressure: Idling	10 to 25 lb./sq. in. (·7 to 1·7 kg./cm.²)
Normal	50 to 80 lb./sq. in. (3·5 to 5 6 kg./cm.²)
Idling setting	500 r.p.m.

Ignition

Static ignition timing: High compression	10° B.T.D.C.
Low compression	8° B.T.D.C.
Stroboscopic ignition timing	14° B.T.D.C. at 600 r.p.m.
Contact breaker gap	·014 to ·016 in. (·36 to ·41 mm.)
Sparking plugs	Champion N–9Y
Plug gap	·025 in. (·64 mm.)

Fuel system

Carburetters	Two S.U. type HS4
Needle	FX.
Fuel pump	S.U. Type HP or AUF 300 electric

Gearbox and overdrive

Overdrive ratio	·802 : 1	
Overall ratios: First	14·214 : 1	
Second	8·656 : 1	*Overdrive*
Third	5·369 : 1	4·306 : 1
Fourth	3·909 : 1	3·135 : 1
Reverse	18·588 : 1	
Top gear speed per 1,000 r.p.m.:		
Standard	17·9 m.p.h. (27·3 km.p.h.)	
Overdrive	22·3 m.p.h. (35·5 km.p.h.)	

Wheels

Type	*Tourer*	*GT*
Ventilated disc	4J × 14	5J × 14
Wire (optional)	4½ × 14 (60-spoke)	

Tyres

	Tourer	*GT*
Standard:		
Size	5·60—14 (tubed C41)	
Optional:	*Tourer*	*GT*
Size	155—14 (SP)	165—14 (SP)

Standard tyres:

	Tourer	GT
Pressures (set cold):		
Front	18 lb./sq. in. (1·3 kg./cm.^{2})	20 lb./sq. in. (1·4 kg./cm.^{2})
Rear	18 lb./sq. in. (1·3 kg./cm.^{2})	24 lb./sq. in. (1·7 kg./cm.^{2})
Sustained speeds in excess of 90 m.p.h. (145 km.p.h.):		
Front	24 lb./sq. in. (1·7 kg./cm.^{2})	26 lb./sq. in. (1·8 kg./cm.^{2})
Rear	24 lb./sq. in. (1·7 kg./cm.^{2})	30 lb./sq. in. (2·1 kg./cm.^{2})

Optional tyres (SP):

	Tourer	GT
Pressures (set cold):		
Front	21 lb./sq. in. (1·5 kg./cm.^{2})	21 lb./sq. in. (1·5 kg./cm.^{2})
Rear	24 lb./sq. in. (1·7 kg./cm.^{2})	24 lb./sq. in. (1·7 kg./cm.^{2})
Sustained speeds in excess of 90 m.p.h. (145 km.p.h.):		
Front	27 lb./sq. in. (1·9 kg./cm.^{2})	28 lb./sq. in. (2·0 kg./cm.^{2})
Rear	31 lb./sq. in. (2·2 kg./cm.^{2})	31 lb./sq. in. (2·2 kg./cm.^{2})

NOTE.—Rear tyre pressures should be increased by 2 lb./sq. in. (·14 kg./cm.^{2}) when touring with a full luggage compartment.

Capacities

Fuel tank:	
Early Tourer cars	10 gallons (45·4 litres, 12 U.S. gal.)
Later Tourer and GT cars	12 gallons (54 litres, 14 U.S. gal.)
Cooling system	9½ pints (5·4 litres, 11·4 U.S. pints)
Cooling system with heater	10 pints (5·6 litres, 12 U.S. pints)
Sump	7½ pints (4·26 litres, 9 U.S. pints)
Oil cooler (when fitted)	¾ pint (·42 litre, ·9 U.S. pint)
Gearbox	4½ pints (2·56 litres, 5·6 U.S. pints)
Gearbox and overdrive	5¼ pints (3·0 litres, 6 U.S. pints)
Rear axle:	
Tourer	2¼ pints (1·3 litres, 2·7 U.S. pints)
GT	1½ pints (·85 litres, 2 U.S. pints)

Dimensions

Length (overall)	12 ft. 8½ in. (3·8 m.)
Length (overall) with over-riders	12 ft. 9⁷⁄₁₆ in. (3·9 m.)
Width (overall)	4 ft. 11¹⁵⁄₁₆ in. (152·3 cm.)
Height (overall), hood erected	4 ft. 1⅜ in. (125·4 cm.)
Ground clearance (minimum)	5 in. (12·7 cm.)

GENERAL DATA

Track: Front:	Disc wheels	..	..	4 ft. 1 in. (124·4 cm.)	
	Wire wheels	..	..	4 ft. 1¼ in. (125·0 cm.)	
Rear:	Disc wheels	..	..	4 ft. 1¼ in. (125·0 cm.)	
	Wire wheels	..	..	4 ft. 1¼ in. (125·0 cm.)	
Wheelbase	..	..	..	7 ft. 7 in. (231·1 cm.)	
Turning circle	..	..	..	32 ft. (9·75 m.)	
Toe-in	..	..	..	$\frac{1}{16}$ to $\frac{3}{32}$ in. (1·5 to 2·3 mm.)	

Weights				*Tourer*	*GT*
Unladen	..	..	..	1,920 lb. (871 kg.)	2,190 lb. (993 kg.)
Kerbside	..	..	..	2,030 lb. (920 kg.)	2,310 lb. (1048 kg.)
Max. permissible gross		..	..	2,430 lb. (1102 kg.)	2,660 lb. (1206 kg.)

IDENTIFICATION

When communicating with your Distributor or Dealer always quote the car and engine numbers. When the communication concerns the transmission units or body details it is necessary to quote also the transmission casing and body numbers.

Car number. Stamped on a plate secured to the top left-hand side of the front bulkhead.

Engine number. On a metal plate fixed to the right-hand side of the cylinder block.

Gearbox number. Stamped on the top of the gearbox to the left of the dipstick and filler plug.

Rear axle number. Stamped on the front of the axle tube on the left-hand side adjacent to the spring seat.

Ignition key number. To reduce the possibility of theft ignition switches are not marked with a number. Owners are advised to make a note of the number appearing on the ignition key in case of loss.

NOTE.—References to right- or left-hand in this Handbook are made when viewing the car from the rear.

Tuning modifications

For competition use or improved road performance, a wide range of BMC Special Tuning parts are available through your BMC Dealer or Distributor. Full details are given in Tuning Booklet C–AKD 4034 of varying stages of tune, as well as wide rim wheels, competition pads and brake linings, close-ratio gears, alternative axle ratios, fly-off hand brake parts, special hard setting shock absorbers, and stiffer anti-roll bars.

The 'MGB' as delivered from the Factory in its standard form is tuned to give maximum performance with complete reliability, and any increase in power must inevitably tend to reduce reliability. For this reason, the terms of the Warranty on a new M.G. expressly exclude any super-tuning of this nature.

CONTROLS AND INSTRUMENTS

Hand brake

The hand brake is of the pull-up lever type, operating mechanically on the rear wheels only. To release the hand brake, pull it upwards to take the load, press the ratchet release button located in the end of the lever with the thumb and push the lever down into the 'off' position. The hand brake is automatically adjusted at the same time as the foot brake and requires no separate adjustment.

Pedals

The left-hand pedal operates the clutch, the centre pedal the brakes, and the right-hand pedal the accelerator. Keep the foot clear of the clutch pedal except when engagement or disengagement of any gear is intended, or when in heavy traffic. Driving with the foot resting on the pedal will lead to rapid clutch wear.

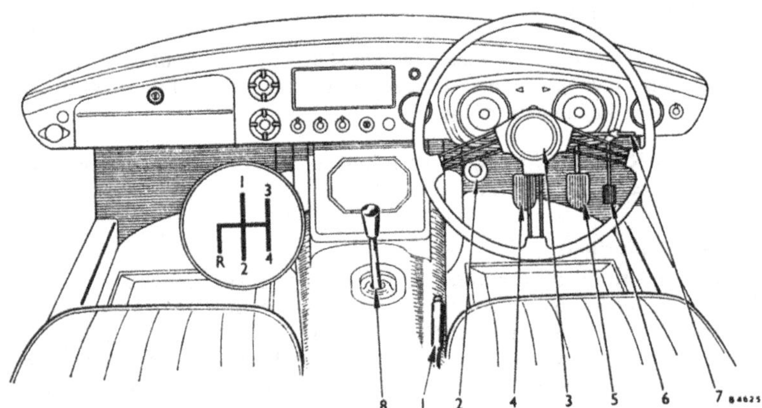

Driving controls—right-hand drive

1. Hand brake.	5. Brake pedal.
2. Headlight dip switch.	6. Accelerator pedal.
3. Horn switch.	7. Direction indicator.
4. Clutch pedal.	8. Gear lever.

Gear lever

The four forward gears and the reverse gear are engaged by moving the lever to the positions illustrated.

To engage reverse gear move the lever to the left of the neutral position until resistance is felt, apply side pressure to the lever to overcome resistance and then pull it backwards to engage the gear.

Synchromesh engagement is provided on second, third and fourth gears.

Always ensure that the gear lever is in the neutral position before attempting to start the engine.

Horn switch

The horns are sounded by a horn-push located in the steering-wheel hub.

Ignition and starter switch

The ignition and starter are both controlled by a single switch operated by a removable key. To switch on the ignition insert the key and turn it in a clockwise direction until a slight resistance is felt. Further movement in the same direction will operate the starter motor. Release the key immediately the engine starts. If the engine fails to start first time wait until it has come to rest before using the starter again.

Headlight beam dipping switch

The headlight main-beam dipping switch is located on the toeboard to the left of the clutch pedal. It is of the single-acting repeating type, lowering the beams on one application and raising them on the next. A warning light on the face of the speedometer glows when the beams are in the raised position.

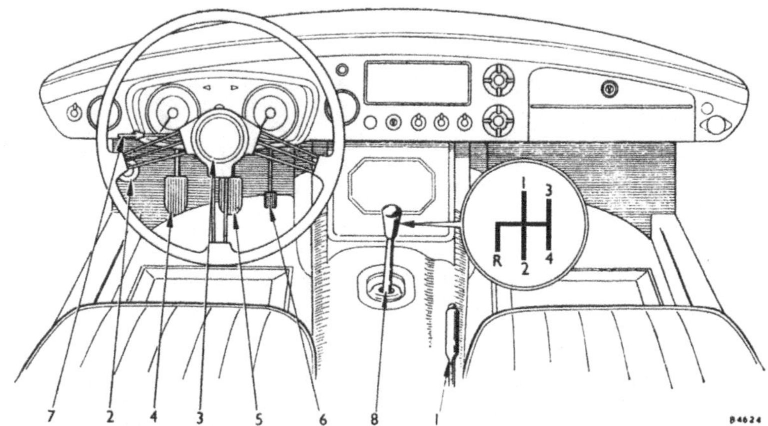

Driving controls—left-hand drive

1. Hand brake.
2. Headlight dip switch.
3. Horn switch.
4. Clutch pedal.
5. Brake pedal.
6. Accelerator pedal.
7. Direction indicator.
8. Gear lever.

Choke or mixture control

To enrich the mixture and assist starting when the engine is cold pull out the knob marked 'C'. The control, when turned half a turn clockwise, will hold in any position, giving a progressively richer mixture as it is pulled out.

On no account should the engine run for any length of time with the knob pulled fully out. It should be returned to the 'off' position (pushed in) as soon as possible as the engine warms up.

The first $\frac{1}{4}$ in. (6 mm.) approx. of movement operates only the throttle control. This initial movement can be used to give a fast engine idling speed and prevent stalling when driving at low speeds before the engine has fully warmed up.

Heater and ventilating controls

These controls provide a means of regulating the heating and ventilating system. Full operating instructions are given on page 13.

CONTROLS AND INSTRUMENTS

Ignition warning light

The ignition warning light serves the dual purpose of reminding the driver to switch off the ignition, and of acting as a no-charge indicator. With the ignition switched on the warning light should only be illuminated when the engine is not running, or is running at a very low speed. As the engine speed increases the light should dim and then go out at a fairly low engine speed.

If the light fails to go out until higher engine speeds are reached or remains alight at all times, inspect the dynamo driving belt for correct tension or breakage.

If the belt is in order the charging system must be overhauled by a Distributor or Dealer.

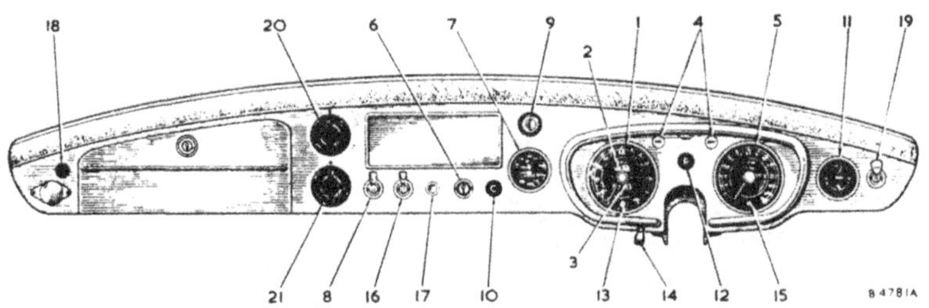

Instruments and switches—right-hand drive

1. Speedometer.
2. Trip mileage indicator.
3. Total mileage indicator.
4. Direction indicator warning lights.
5. Tachometer.
6. Ignition and starter switch.
7. Oil pressure and water temperature gauge.
8. Blower switch.
9. Lighting switch.
10. Choke (mixture control).
11. Fuel gauge.
12. Panel light switch.
13. Headlight main-beam warning light.
14. Trip mileage resetting knob.
15. Ignition warning light.
16. Windscreen wiper switch.
17. Windscreen washer.
18. Map light switch.
19. Overdrive switch.
20. Heater control.
21. Air control.

Lighting switch

Earlier cars

A lever-type switch. Move the lever downward to the half-way position for the side and tail lights, and into the fully down position for the headlights.

Later cars

A push/pull switch. Pull out to the first position for the side and tail lights, and fully out for headlights.

Map-reading light switch

The map-reading light is controlled by a switch adjacent to the lamp. The lamp will only operate when the side lights are switched on.

Panel light switch

The panel light switch is located between the speedometer and the engine revolution indicator. To illuminate the instruments turn the knob clockwise. The first movement of the knob switches on the lights and further turning to the right dims them.

The panel lights will only function when the side lights are switched on.

Overdrive switch

The overdrive switch is mounted on the outer edge of the fascia adjacent to the instrument panel. The switch bezel is marked 'NORMAL' and 'OVER-DRIVE'.

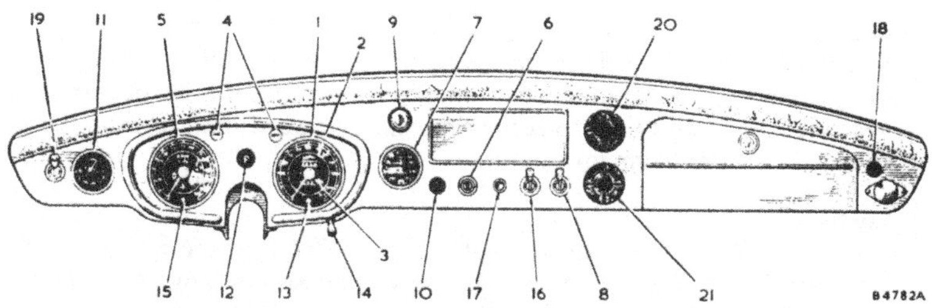

Instruments and switches—left-hand drive

1. Speedometer.
2. Trip mileage indicator.
3. Total mileage indicator.
4. Direction indicator warning lights.
5. Tachometer.
6. Ignition and starter switch.
7. Oil pressure and water temperature gauge.
8. Blower switch.
9. Lighting switch.
10. Choke (mixture control).
11. Fuel gauge.
12. Panel light switch.
13. Headlight main-beam warning light.
14. Trip mileage resetting knob.
15. Ignition warning light.
16. Windscreen wiper switch.
17. Windscreen washer.
18. Map light switch.
19. Overdrive switch.
20. Heater control.
21. Air control.

Oil pressure gauge

The engine oil pressure should be between 50 and 80 lb./sq. in. (3·5 and 5·6 kg./cm.²) under normal running conditions. Approximately 10 to 25 lb./sq. in. (·7 to 1·7 kg./cm.²) should be shown when the engine is idling. Should the gauge fail to register any pressure at all, stop the engine immediately and investigate the cause.

Temperature gauge

When the engine is running the gauge indicates the temperature of the coolant leaving the cylinder head.

As overheating may cause serious damage, the readings should be noted and after the initial rise in temperature during the warming-up period any sudden upward change in the reading calls for immediate investigation.

When the ignition is switched off the needle returns to the 'cold' position.

CONTROLS AND INSTRUMENTS

Fuel gauge

A few seconds after the ignition is switched on the fuel gauge indicates the quantity of fuel in the tank. An important note on filling up with fuel is given on page 29.

Direction indicator and headlight flasher switch

The direction indicator switch is mounted on an arm on the steering-column below the steering-wheel. The indicators operate only when the ignition is switched on, and the indicator warning lights in the instrument panel flash when they are in use.

Lifting the lever towards the steering-wheel flashes the headlight beams on later Tourers and all GT cars.

Speedometer

In addition to recording the road speed this instrument also records the trip and total distances. The trip recorder enables the length of a particular journey to be recorded, and can be set to zero by pushing upwards and turning the knob located beneath the instrument.

Tachometer

This instrument indicates the revolutions per minute of the engine, and this assists the driver to use the most effective engine speed range for maximum performance in any gear (see 'RUNNING INSTRUCTIONS').

Windscreen wiper switch

The two windscreen wiper blades are operated by a lever-type switch. Flick down the switch to start the wiper motor. The blades park automatically when the motor is switched off.

Windscreen washer

To wash the windscreen press the control knob. When following other vehicles, particularly under dirty road conditions, the washer should be operated before the wiper blades are set in motion.

In cold weather, the reservoir should be filled with a mixture of water and recommended washer solvent to prevent the water freezing in the reservoir and on the windscreen.

Do not use radiator anti-freeze solution in the windscreen-washing equipment.

Electrically heated back-light (GT) (optional extra)

The electrically heated back-light is controlled by a 'push/pull' type illuminated switch mounted on the fascia panel in the position normally occupied by the heater blower switch, the blower switch being repositioned on the under side of the fascia panel below the windscreen wiper switch.

The heated back-light will only operate when the ignition is switched on; an indicator lamp in the switch will glow when the switch knob is pulled out to the 'on' position.

Cigar-lighter (optional extra)

Press the knob right in to heat the lighter element. When heated sufficiently the lighter unit will be partially ejected, and it is then ready to be withdrawn for lighting purposes.

HEATING AND VENTILATING

Fresh-air system (standard)

Provision is made for admitting fresh air to the car interior for ventilation.

The fresh air is ducted from the bonnet grille to an air box and passes to the car interior through an air outlet vent on the dash panel.

The fresh-air control is located on the dash panel to the left of the speaker panel. Pull the control to open the vent to one of the two positions.

Heating system (optional)

When a heating and demist unit is fitted, fresh air is ducted from the bonnet grille, through the air box to the heater matrix and then to the demist ducts or to the car interior. Two manually operated spring-loaded air outlet doors are located on the inner foot-well sides to admit air to the interior of the car.

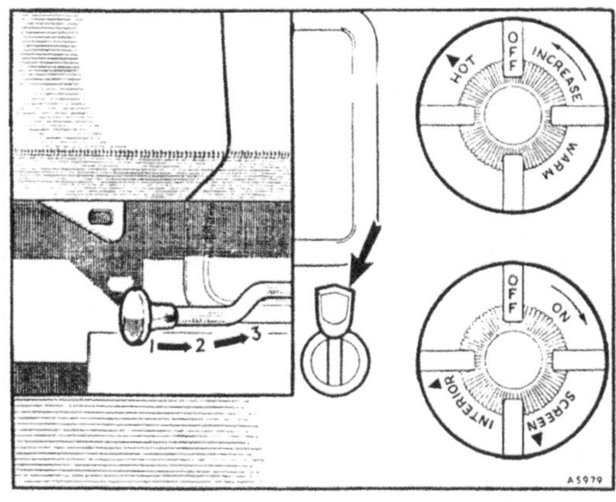

The heater controls and blower switch with the fresh-air control shown inset

The ram effect caused by the forward motion of the car will provide an adequate supply of air above speeds of approximately 25 m.p.h. (40 km.p.h.). An electric blower in the heater unit controlled by a switch on the fascia panel augments the supply when a greater quantity of air is required or when the car is travelling at low speeds or is stationary.

Controls

The upper control operates a water valve connected to the engine cooling system; the valve controls the rate of flow of the hot water to the heater matrix.

Move the control in the direction of the arrow to increase the heat supply to 'WARM' or 'HOT'.

The lower control operates an air flap in the heater outlet box which deflects the air to the screen or to the air outlet doors and car interior.

Turn the control in the direction of the arrow to 'INTERIOR' or 'SCREEN' to deflect air to the car interior or to the windscreen.

Both controls may be set to intermediate positions and thus provide a wide variety of settings to meet varying conditions.

HEATING AND VENTILATING

Use of controls

NOTE.—The full heat output will not be available until the engine has reached its operating temperature.

To obtain maximum heat supply inside the car, turn the air control to 'INTERIOR', the heat control to 'HOT', open the air outlet doors and switch on the blower.

To defrost the windscreen turn the air control to 'SCREEN', the heat control to 'HOT', close the air outlet doors and switch on the blower.

To obtain a supply of unheated fresh air turn the air control to 'INTERIOR', the heat control to 'OFF', open the air outlet doors and switch on the blower.

BODY DETAILS

Bonnet lock

To open the bonnet pull the release inside the car and press up the safety catch. Disengage the bonnet stay from its clip and place the free end in the bracket attached to the front wheel arch.

To close, secure the stay in its clip and lower the bonnet. Apply light pressure with the palms of the hands at the front corners of the bonnet and press down quickly. As the bonnet is aluminium, handle it with care and do not use unnecessary force. The safety catch and lock will be heard to engage.

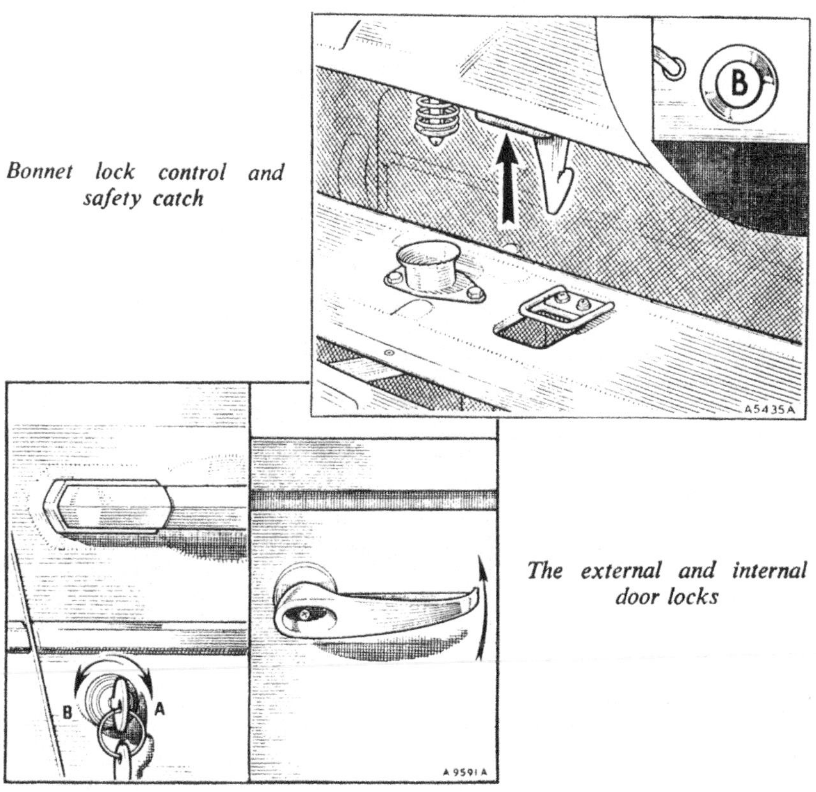

Bonnet lock control and safety catch

The external and internal door locks

Door locks

Both doors may be locked from the outside with the key or from the inside with the internal door handle.

To lock the doors from the outside turn the key slightly towards the front of the car. To unlock the doors turn the key slightly towards the rear of the car. After locking or unlocking the doors return the key to the vertical position and withdraw it.

To lock the doors from inside move the door handle upwards with the minimum amount of pressure to the handle.

Early cars: Only the passenger door may be locked from the inside by turning the locking knob up. Turn the knob down to unlock the door.

BODY DETAILS

Doors

Both doors are provided with door-pulls.

A window regulator handle is fitted to the inside of each door.

A draughtproof ventilator panel adjacent to each window may be opened by releasing the catch.

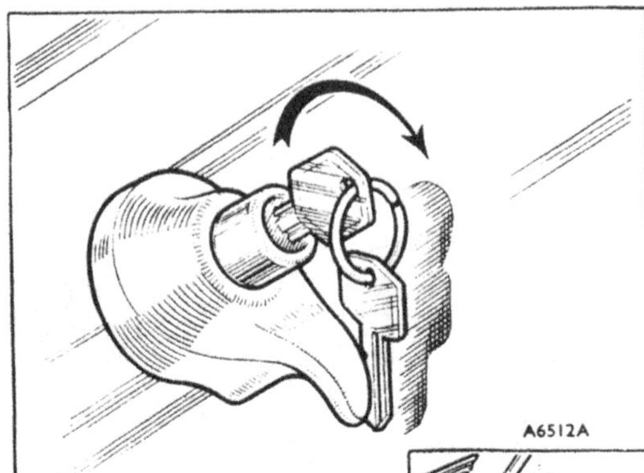

The luggage compartment lock

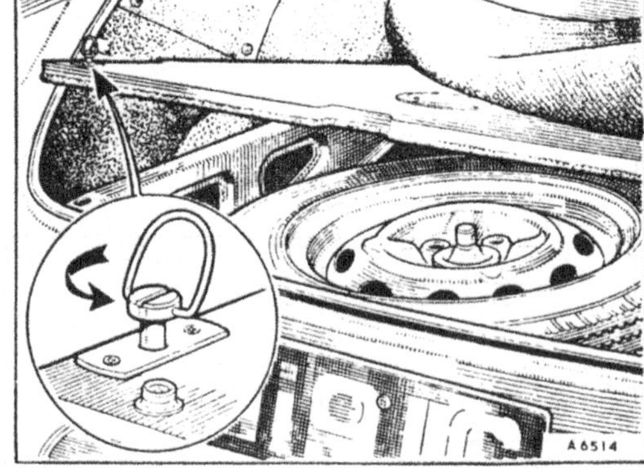

The spare wheel

Luggage compartment

The luggage compartment is locked with the key provided.

Tourer

To open, depress the button catch and raise the lid. Unclip the stay from underneath the lid and secure the free end in the bracket attached to the side of the luggage compartment.

GT

To open, depress the button catch and raise the counterpoised lid.

Spare wheel

The spare wheel is stowed in the luggage compartment.

GT

Turn back the luggage compartment mat and unscrew the quick-release screws. Lift the luggage compartment floor.

Tourer and GT

Unscrew the clamp plate bolt, and lift out the spare wheel.

Seat adjustment

Both front seats are adjustable and may be moved forwards or backwards. To adjust a seat, move the seat catch outwards, slide the seat to the required position and ensure that the catch engages the nearest slot in the seat runner.

The seat squabs are also adjustable for rake by loosening the squab to frame bracket securing screw, loosening the two adjusting screw locknuts and then adjusting the screws.

After adjustment lock the screws with their locknuts and tighten the bracket screw.

The bracket may be reversed to enable the seat squab to tip for the purpose of loading or unloading luggage into the rear cockpit.

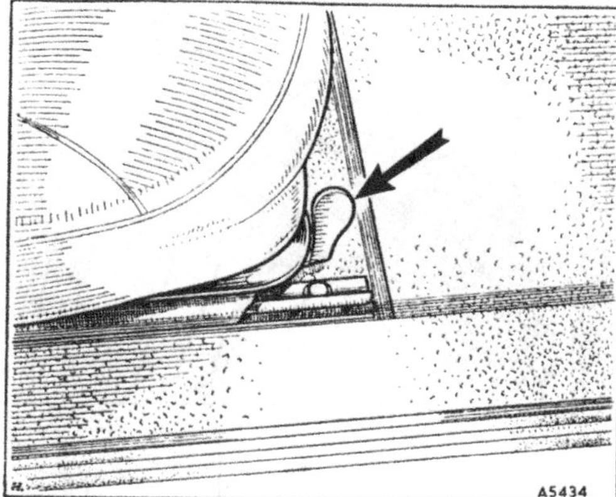

A seat catch and slide

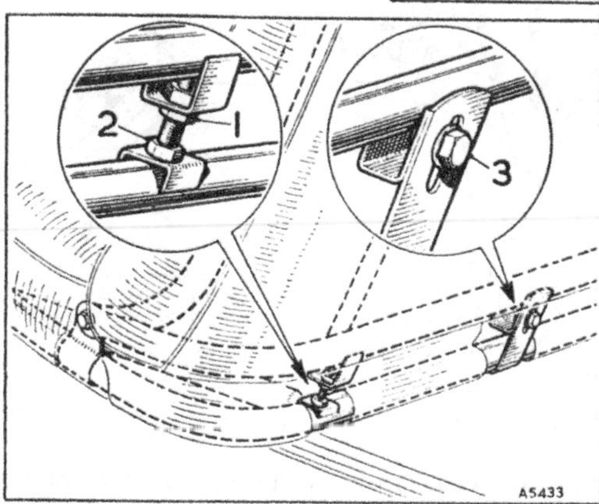

A seat squab, showing:

1. Adjusting screw locknut.
2. Adjusting screw.
3. Bracket securing screw.

Glovebox

The glovebox is located on the passenger's side of the fascia panel and can be locked with a separate key.

Fuel filler

The fuel filler pipe is fitted with a bayonet-type filler cap which may be removed by turning it in an anti-clockwise direction.

BODY DETAILS

Hood (standard)

Erecting the hood

Remove the hood from its stowed position (see page 19).

Erect the collapsible frame and pull the front stick forward; leave the rear stick in the collapsed position until the canopy is fitted.

Place the ends of the frame in the support sockets that are fitted one to each rear quarter panel. The long stick faces forward.

The hood sticks fitted and erected

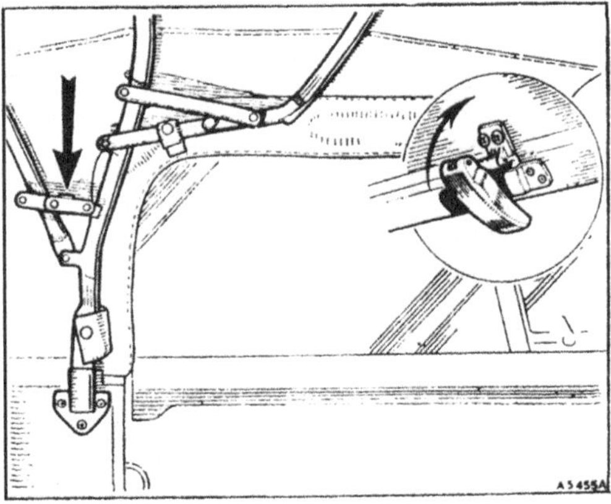

Extend the rear stick and ensure that the links (one shown arrowed) pass over their centres, inset is the windscreen toggle catches

Unfold the hood over the frame and engage the two locating sockets on the lower rear edge of the canopy with the retaining plates on the rear tonneau panel. Engage the hood quarter panel retainers in the locating sockets to the rear of each door opening. Engage the fasteners around the rear edge of the canopy. Secure the hood header rail to the windscreen frame with the toggle lever catches and the two fastener assemblies.

Extend the rear stick to tension the canopy and ensure that the connecting links pass over their centres. Then secure the hood **to** the foot of each socket and the rear quarter of the frame linkages.

Removing the hood

Unlock the over-centre links on the rear stick to slacken the canopy. Undo the fasteners and release the toggle lever catches on the windscreen. Release all fasteners around the rear of the hood and the retainers to the rear of each door opening. Slide the rear hood rail backwards clear of the two slotted fasteners on the tonneau panel, and lift the hood from the frame.

NOTE.—It is most important that the instructions given should be followed when folding and stowing the hood in order to obviate damage to the quarter- and back-lights. Never fold the hood when it is wet or damp.

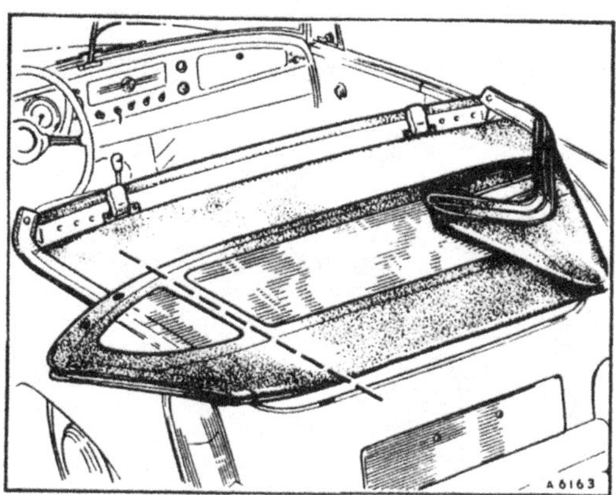

Fold the quarter-lights inwards, folding on a line between the quarter-light and back-light

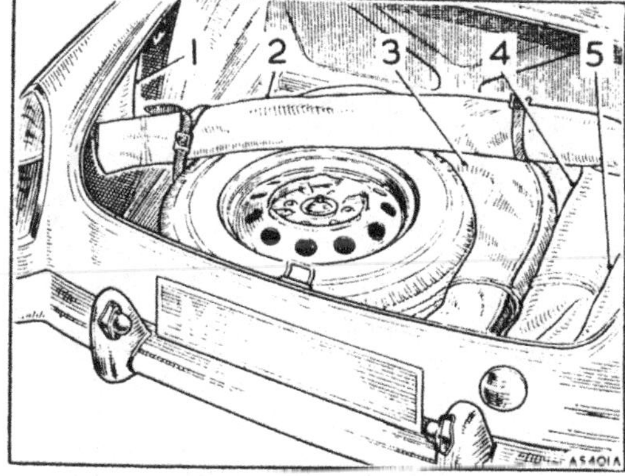

The luggage compartment, showing the stowage positions for:

1. Tonneau rail.
2. Standard hood canopy.
3. Hood frame.
4. Tool bag.
5. Tonneau cover and hood cover.

Folding the hood

Folding the hood correctly is of utmost importance; lay the hood on a flat surface with the lining upwards. Fold the hood in the way shown in the illustration and then roll it up carefully, avoiding kinking.

Stowing the hood and hood sticks

Withdraw the frame from the support sockets, fold the sticks and separate the two halves of the frame. Place the canopy and the frame in their respective stowage bags and stow in the luggage compartment.

The hood may suffer damage if stowed without the protection of stowage bag.

BODY DETAILS

Hood (optional)

Removing the hood cover

To remove the hood cover undo the two lift-dot fasteners on one of the inner side panels of the rear cockpit, release the four fasteners from the rear quarter-panel, and disengage the hood clip from its socket. Release the other side in a similar manner.

Disengage the back of the cover from the anchor plates on the rear tonneau panel, remove and fold the cover, and place it in its stowage bag.

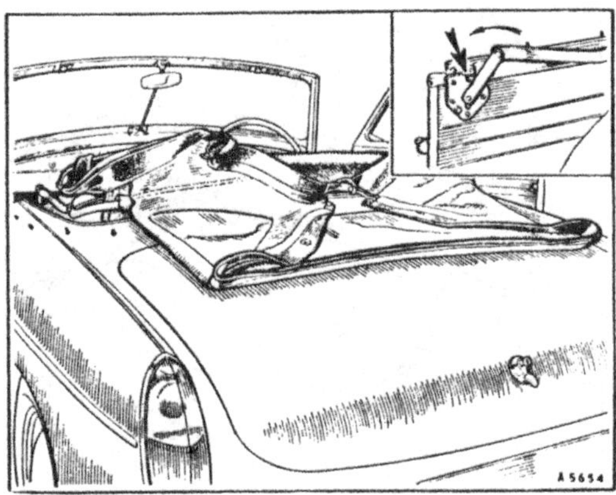

Lift the hood from the rear cockpit and lay it on the tonneau panel. Engage the swivel links (inset) in their respective slots and unroll the back-light (early models only)

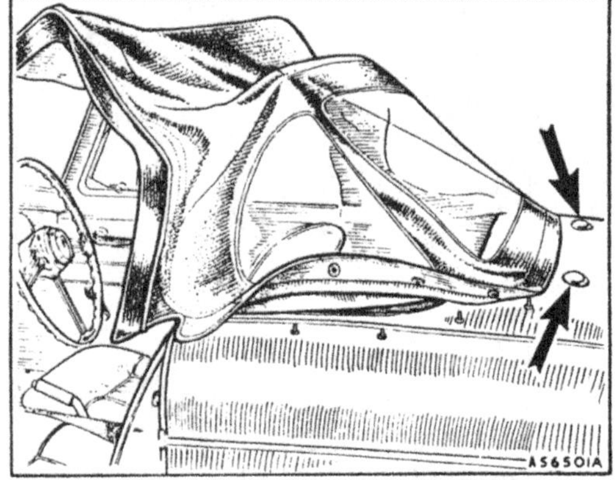

Lift the hood and engage the bottom of the back-light in the anchor plates on the tonneau panel. Pull the hood forward and engage the hood clips and then do up the four fasteners on the rear quarter-panel

Remove and dismantle the tonneau rail and place it in its stowage bag. Stow the cover and rail in the luggage compartment.

Raising the hood

To raise the hood, release the hood-securing straps, lift the hood from the rear cockpit, and pull it back onto the tonneau panel. Alternatively, lower the seat squabs (this is only possible when the squab-retaining brackets have been reversed) and swing the hood forward until it rests on the rear of the seat squabs.

Pivot each swivel link in turn to its upper position and drop them into their respective slots in the base of the hood frame fitting (early models).

Lift the hood from the seat squabs or tonneau panel and allow the back-light to unroll. Engage the bottom of the back-light in the anchor plates on the tonneau panel and pull the header rail forward to prevent the hood falling backwards.

Unfold a quarter-light, engage the hood clip in its socket, and then do up the four fasteners on the quarter-panel. Secure the other quarter-light in a similar manner.

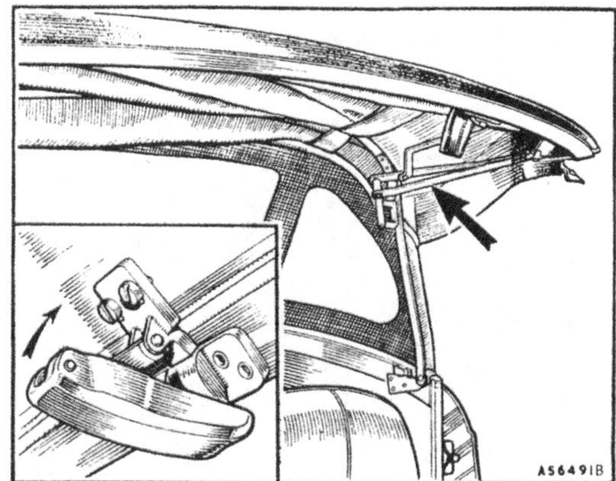

Extend the hinge links and (inset) do up the toggle fasteners

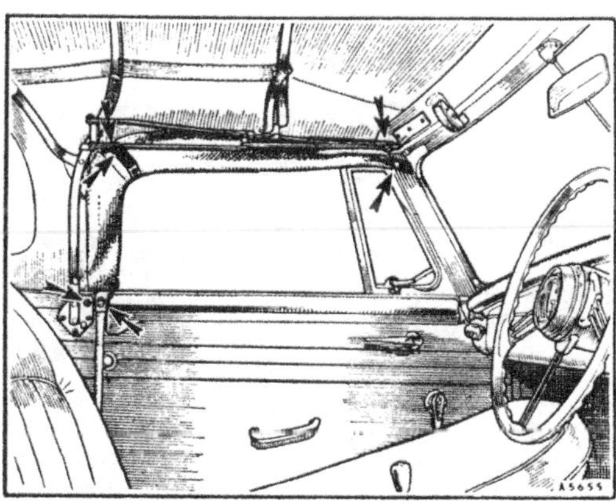

Do up the six lift-dot fasteners (three shown arrowed)

From inside the car fully extend the hinge links and engage the toggle fasteners on the header rail with their sockets on the top of the windscreen frame.

Secure the six lift-dot fasteners situated one at the top of each windscreen pillar, one on the rear of each hinge link, and one on each swivel link.

Link each of the two hood-retaining straps together.

BODY DETAILS

Lowering the hood

Never fold the hood when it is wet or damp.

From inside the car release the six lift-dot fasteners and the toggle fasteners. Lift the header rail clear of the windscreen frame and then collapse the hinge links.

On one side of the car release the four fasteners on the rear quarter-panel, disengage the hood clip, and fold the quarter-light onto the back-light; ensure that the fold is made along the hood material, continue this fold along the side edge of the hood to the front.

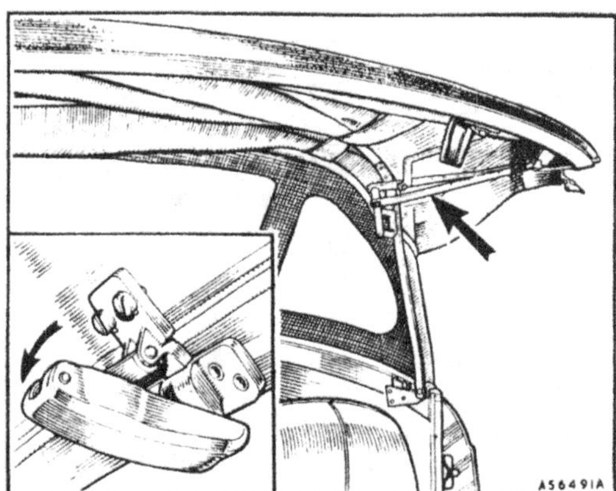

Undo the six lift-dot fasteners, release the toggle fasteners, and collapse the hinge links

Fold the quarter-lights and side overhang inwards, release the back-light from the anchor plates, and lay the hood on the tonneau panel or rear of the seat squabs. Roll up the back-light and cover it with the surplus canopy. Then disengage the swivel links (later cars)

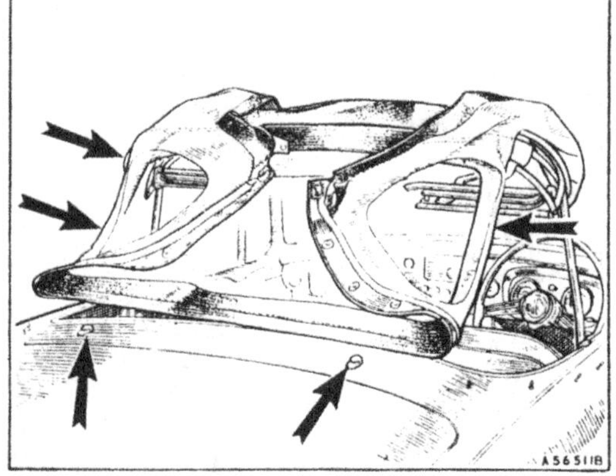

From the other side of the car release and fold the remaining quarter-light and side overhang in a similar manner.

Bring the header rail towards the rear frame and pull out the surplus hood material clear of the frame. Support the hood with one hand and with the other release the bottom of the hood from the anchor plates. Allow the hood to rest on the tonneau panel or the rear of the seat squabs.

Disengage each swivel link in turn (early models) and then roll up the back-light and quarter-lights. Fold the surplus canopy over the back-light to protect it.

Lift the hood from the rear of the seat squabs or the tonneau panel and pivot it down into the rear cockpit. Pull the hood back as far as it will go (early models) and secure it with the two straps.

Fitting the hood cover

Assemble the tonneau rail and fit it to the body sockets with the cross-rod of the rail towards the rear. Spread the cover over the rail and engage the back of the cover with the anchor plates on the tonneau panel. Engage the hood cover clip with its socket and do up the four fasteners on the rear quarter panel. Do up the two lift-dot fasteners inside the rear cockpit.

Secure the other side of the hood cover in a similar manner.

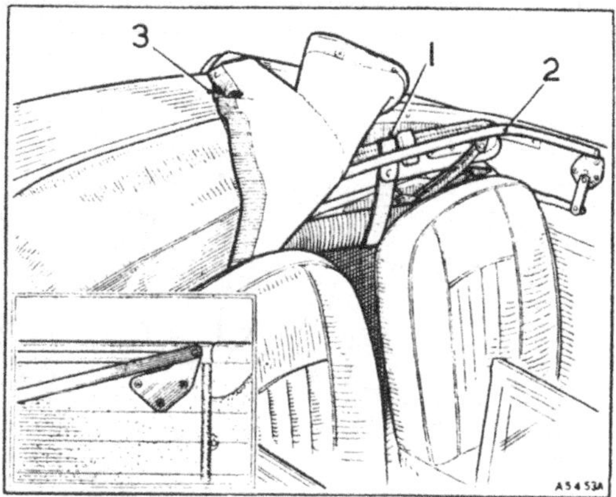

The optional hood in the stowed position, showing:

1. A hood securing strap.
2. The tonneau rail.
3. Hood cover.

Inset: later type head stick

The tonneau cover fitted, with the cover from the driving position folded down behind the seat and secured to the heelboard

Tonneau cover

Fitting

Remove the tonneau cover and rail from its stowed position in the luggage compartment. Assemble the rail into the existing hood stick sockets. Engage the rear edge of the cover with the retaining plates and fasteners on the tonneau and quarter panels.

BODY DETAILS

Extend the cover forward to cover the seats and attach the front of the cover to the fasteners on the fascia panel top.

The front of the cover may be unzipped and folded back to give access to the driver's seat or folded back to give access to both front seats. When folded back ensure that the cover is folded under and that the flaps are securely attached to the fasteners on the heelboard.

Zip fasteners in the cover behind the tonneau rail permit seat belts to be used when the cover is in the folded-back position. Ensure that the flaps adjacent to these fasteners are secured.

Removing

When removing the tonneau cover reverse the fitting procedure. Dismantle the tonneau cover rail, fold the tonneau cover and stow it in the luggage compartment.

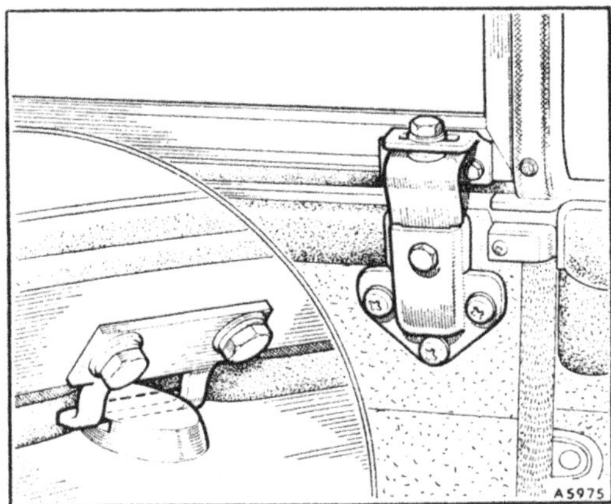

One of the two hard top fixing brackets and the rear anchor bracket shown inset

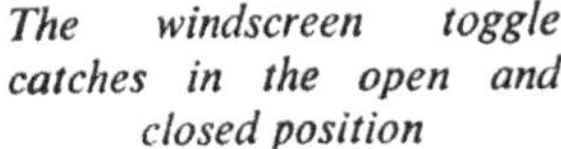

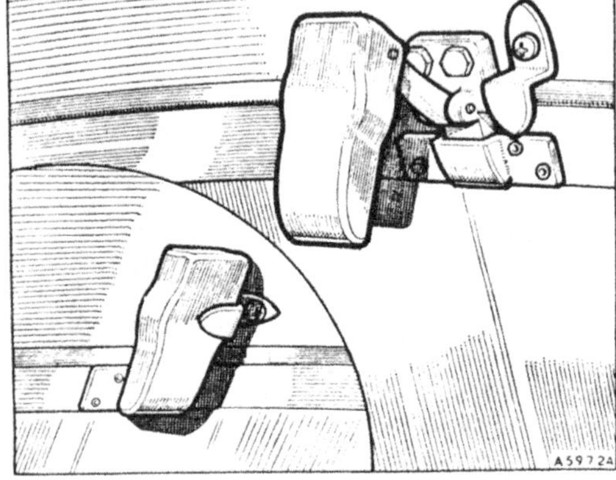

The windscreen toggle catches in the open and closed position

Hard top

Fitting

Assemble the quarter panel side brackets to the side sockets on the car, using a spring washer under the head of the bolt. Tighten the single bolt securing each bracket and remove the hard top securing bolts complete with their four washers; keep these ready to hand.

With one person at each side, lift the hard top into position over the rear of the car.

Lower the rear end of the hard top and engage the anchor plate brackets with the car anchor plates. Difficulty will be met if the rear sealing rubber is not clear of the anchor plate brackets.

Centralize the hard top to the car by lining up the hard top drip moulding with the rear wing top beading.

Apply hand pressure evenly to the rear of the hard top and check that the front toggle fastener tongues are in their sockets on the windscreen with the front sealing rubber forward of the windscreen top. In this position, with pressure still applied from the rear, insert the quarter panel side bracket bolts, one each side with one washer under the head of the bolt and the other three between the bracket on the hard top and the bracket on the side socket of the car. **DO NOT TIGHTEN THE BOLTS DOWN FULLY AT THIS STAGE.**

Centralize the hard top onto the windscreen and ensure that the front sealing rubber fits down snugly and evenly. With the hard top pushed forward as far as possible, adjust the front toggle links to give an adequate tension to the over-centre action; this is achieved by trial. Tighten the bolts securing the toggles to the hard top. Fasten the toggle links and apply the safety catches.

Loosen the hard top side securing bolts and check that the quarter panel sealing rubber is correctly positioned to pull down onto the car body.

Whilst pressing down on the rear of the hard top, examine the gap between the two side brackets. Determine the quantity of washers necessary to fill this gap and fit one less than this. Repeat this on the other side of the car.

Keeping the rest of the hard top centralized tighten the hard top side securing bolts fully. With pressure applied downwards on the rear of the hard top, tighten the anchor plate securing bolts.

Final check of the correct hard top position is obtained by winding up the door windows. A gap of approximately $\frac{5}{16}$ in. (7·9 mm.) should exist between the rear vertical edge of the door windows and the quarter light channel, adjustment may be achieved by loosening the side securing bolts and moving the hard top forward or to the rear as required. Check also that an even and adequate seal is made between the window and the hard top rubber. Retighten the side securing bolts and carefully check the door opening and closing actions.

Removing

Release the toggle fastener safety catches by unscrewing the Phillips-headed screws. Swing the catches clear of the fasteners and release the toggles.

Remove the bolts, complete with washers, securing the hard top to the quarter panel side brackets.

Loosen the bolts securing the rear anchor plate brackets to the hard top.

Raise the front of the hard top to clear the toggle fastener tongues, move the hard top to the rear to disengage the anchor plates, and lift it clear of the car.

Remove the quarter panel side brackets from their sockets on the car and stow them in the inverted position on the hard top complete with fixing bolts and washers.

BODY DETAILS

Vent windows

To open, pull the catch forward and push outwards. Close the window by pulling the centre of the catch inwards and then pushing backwards until the catch is felt to snap over into the locked position.

The rear ventilator window toggle catch

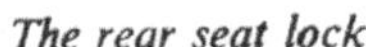

The rear seat lock

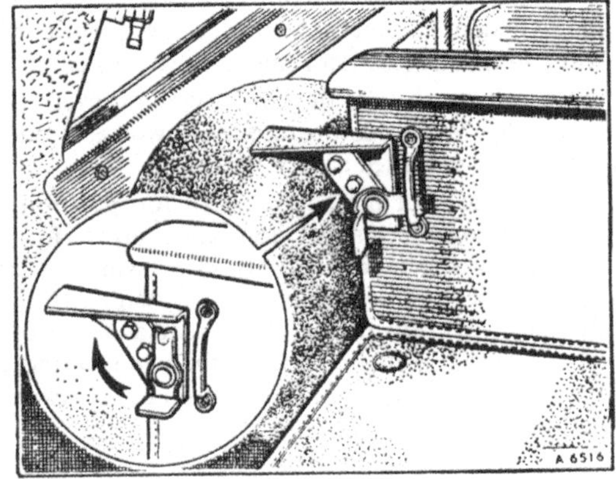

Rear seat (increased luggage capacity)

Release the lock, and pull the seat forward at the top, and lower it until the floor is level. A ledge is provided at the top of the seat to stop the luggage moving forward during heavy braking.

Seat belts

Seat belts are obtainable from authorized Distributors and Dealers, and should only be fitted by them to the attachment points incorporated in the body structure.

The approved 'Kangol Magnet' belts consist of a long belt attached at one end to the rear wheel arch and the other end to the sill, and a short belt attached to the side of the drive shaft tunnel farthest from the wearer.

A driver's seat belt

To fasten—lift up the magnetic buckle tongue and engage the hook into the hinged part of the tongue.

To release—lift the magnetic buckle tongue.

To adjust—tighten the short belt with the adjuster at the buckle until the buckle rests on the side of the hip (see illustration). With the adjuster at the sill tighten the belt until lap belt fits comfortably and a hand clearance between the diagonal belt and the chest is just possible. Slight readjustment may be necessary during use.

To stow—hook the buckle on the long belt into the slot in the stowing bracket mounted under the hood centre locating socket. Attach the magnetic buckle on the short belt to the seat frame.

BODY ATTENTION

Coachwork

Regular care of the body finish is necessary if the new appearance of the car exterior is to be maintained against the effects of air pollution, rain, and mud.

Wash the bodywork frequently, using a soft sponge and plenty of water containing a mild detergent. Large deposits of mud must be softened with water before using the sponge. Smears should be removed by a second wash in clean water, and with the sponge if necessary. When dry, clean the surface of the car with a damp chamois-leather. In addition to the regular maintenance, special attention is required if the car is driven in extreme conditions such as sea spray or on salted roads. In these conditions and with other forms of severe contamination an additional washing operation is necessary, which should include under-body hosing. Any damaged areas should be immediately covered with paint and a complete repair effected as soon as possible. Before touching-in light scratches and abrasions with paint thoroughly clean the surface. Use petrol/white spirit (gasoline/hydrocarbon solvent) to remove spots of grease or tar.

The application of BMC Car Polish is all that is required to remove traffic film and to ensure the retention of the new appearance.

Bright trim

Never use an abrasive on stainless, chromium, aluminium, or bright plastic parts, and on no account clean them with metal polish. Remove spots of grease or tar with petrol/white spirit (gasoline/hydrocarbon solvent) and wash frequently with water containing a mild detergent. When the dirt has been removed polish with a clean dry cloth or chamois-leather until bright. Any slight tarnish found on stainless or plated components which have not received regular attention may be removed with BMC Chrome Cleaner. An occasional application of mineral light oil or grease will help to preserve the finish, particularly during winter, when salt may be used on the roads, but these protectives must not be applied to plastic finishes.

Windscreen

If smearing has occurred it can be removed with BMC Screen Cleaner.

Interior

Clean the carpets with a stiff brush or vacuum cleaner, preferably before washing the outside of the car. The most satisfactory way to give carpets a thorough cleaning is to apply BMC 2-way Cleaner with a semi-stiff brush, brush vigorously and remove the surplus with a damp cloth or sponge. Carpets should not be cleaned by the 'Dry-Clean' process. The upholstery and roof lining may be treated with BMC 2-way Cleaner applied with a damp cloth and a light rubbing action.

A razor blade will remove transfers from the window glass.

Cleaning the hood

To clean the hood it is only necessary to use soap and water, with a soft brush to remove any ingrained dirt. Frequent washing with soap and water considerably improves the appearance and wearing qualities of the hood, and it should be washed at least as often as the rest of the car.

Do not use caustic soaps, detergents, or spirit cleaners to clean the hood or the hood back-light.

The BMC-approved products mentioned above are obtainable from your Distributor or Dealer.

RUNNING INSTRUCTIONS

Starting

Before starting the engine ensure that the gear lever is in neutral and the hand brake is applied. If the engine is cold pull out the choke control.

Switch on the ignition, ensure that the ignition warning light glows and that the fuel gauge registers, then operate the starter. Release it if the engine fails to start within five or six seconds, wait for the crankshaft to stop rotating, and then operate the starter again.

Should the engine fail to start after a reasonable number of attempts, check for possible causes.

The continued use of the starter when the engine fails to start will not only discharge the battery but also damage the starter.

If the pinion fails to disengage when the engine starts the starter will emit a high-pitched whine and the engine must be stopped immediately.

As soon as the engine starts, release the starter and warm up the engine at a fairly fast idling speed. Should the oil gauge fail to register any pressure or if the pressure is very low, stop the engine immediately and investigate the cause. Failure to do so may result in serious damage to the engine. Also check that the ignition warning light goes out when the engine is running above idling speed; failure of the light to behave in this fashion indicates a broken fan belt or other fault in the system.

Push in the mixture control knob completely as soon as the engine will run evenly without its use.

Warming up

Research has proved that the practice of warming up an engine by allowing it to idle slowly is definitely harmful. The correct procedure is to let the engine run fairly fast, at approximately 1,000 r.p.m., corresponding to a speed of about 18 m.p.h. (27 km.p.h.) in top gear, so that it attains its correct working temperature **as quickly as possible**. Allowing the engine to work slowly in a cold state leads to excessive cylinder wear, and far less damage is done by driving the car straight on the road from cold than by letting the engine idle slowly in the garage.

Wet brakes

When the vehicle is being washed or driven through water the brake linings may become wet. To dry them, apply the brakes several times with the vehicle moving slowly. Driving with wet brakes can be dangerous.

Filling up with fuel

When filling up with fuel avoid filling the tank until fuel is visible in the filler intake tube. Should this be done and the car left in the sun, there will be a considerable risk of fuel leakage due to expansion, and consequent danger from exposed fuel. If inadvertently overfilled, take care to park the car in the shade with the filler intake as high as possible.

Running in

The treatment given to a new car will have an important bearing on its subsequent life, and engine speeds during this early period must be limited. The following instructions should be strictly adhered to.

RUNNING INSTRUCTIONS

During the first 500 miles (800 km.)

DO NOT exceed 45 m.p.h. (72 km.p.h.).
DO NOT operate at full throttle in any gear.
DO NOT allow the engine to labour in any gear.

Tachometer

For normal road work, and to obtain the most satisfactory service from your engine, select the appropriate gear to maintain engine speeds of between 2,000 and 4,500 r.p.m.

When maximum acceleration is required, upward gear selections should be made when the needle reaches the yellow sector (5,500–6,000 r.p.m.). Prolonged or excessive use of the highest engine speeds will tend to shorten the life of the engine. Allowing the engine to pull hard at low engine speeds must be avoided as this also has a detrimental effect on the engine.

The beginning of the red sector (6,000 r.p.m.) indicates the maximum safe speed for the engine. **Never allow the needle to enter the red sector.**

Overdrive (optional)

The overdrive can be engaged at any speed within the third or fourth gear range at any throttle opening between light and full throttle. **DO NOT** depress the clutch pedal to select 'overdrive' or 'normal'.

To prevent overspeeding the engine **DO NOT** select 'normal' top from 'overdrive' top at speeds in excess of the direct drive maximum or change from 'overdrive' third to 'normal' third at speeds in excess of 'normal' third speed maximum.

If increased acceleration is required when in 'overdrive' top the overdrive can be switched out to give normal top gear.

Towing eye

If it is necessary to tow the car, use the towing eye provided on the front cross-member.

High-compression engine (8·8 : 1)

This engine is a highly developed unit and it is essential that you should know something about the specialized maintenance it requires if you are to maintain it at the peak of its mechanical efficiency. Special recommendations on the sparking plugs, ignition settings, and fuel to be used are given by the manufacturers, and it is stressed that failures are bound to occur if these are not strictly adhered to. Particular care is needed with this engine owing to its high compression ratio, which makes it extremely sensitive to variations in fuel, ignition timing, and the heat range of the sparking plugs.

In lower-compression engines a much wider range of fuels can be tolerated without causing serious damage to the engine, and ignition settings will stand variations of a reasonable amount. Also, even if the incorrect sparking plugs are used, no more damage may be incurred than burnt-out plugs or leaky valves. But with an engine having a very high compression ratio the range of fuels, sparking plugs, and ignition settings is much narrower and it is essential that the mixture should always be correct, and particularly never overweak at maximum load or power.

High-compression engines are very sensitive to variations in spark advance (over-advance) and to fuel/air ratio (mixture). Variations in these settings will increase the combustion temperature, and if the variation is excessive pre-ignition will cause high shock waves, resulting in damage to the engine.

The engine should be decarbonized at regular intervals as excessive deposits of ash from the combustion of lubricating oil and fuel can cause pre-ignition difficulties.

Choice of fuel

When fitted with H.C. engine (compression ratio 8·8 : 1)

The octane number of a motor fuel is an indication given by the fuel technicians of its knock resistance. High-octane fuels have been produced to improve the efficiency of engines by allowing them to operate on high compression ratios, resulting in better fuel economy and greater power. Owing to the high compression ratio of the engine, fuels with an octane rating **below 98** are **not** suitable; should it be necessary to use a fuel with a lower octane number, the car must be used very carefully until the correct fuel can be obtained.

It is necessary to use Super grade fuels in the 100-octane range unless premium fuels of minimum 98-octane (Research method) are available.

When fitted with L.C. engine (compression ratio 8·0 : 1)

Premium fuels of minimum 93-octane (Research method) up to 97-octane are required, with preference to 95/97.

Super grade fuels in the 100-octane range can be used if preferred.

COOLING SYSTEM

A pressurized cooling system is used on this vehicle and the pressure must be released gradually when removing the radiator filler cap while the system is hot. It is advisable to protect the hands against escaping steam and then turn the cap slowly anti-clockwise until the resistance of the safety stop is felt. Leave the cap in this position until all pressure is released. Press the cap downwards against the spring to clear the safety stops and continue turning until it can be lifted off.

The radiator drain tap on the left-hand side of the radiator bottom tank

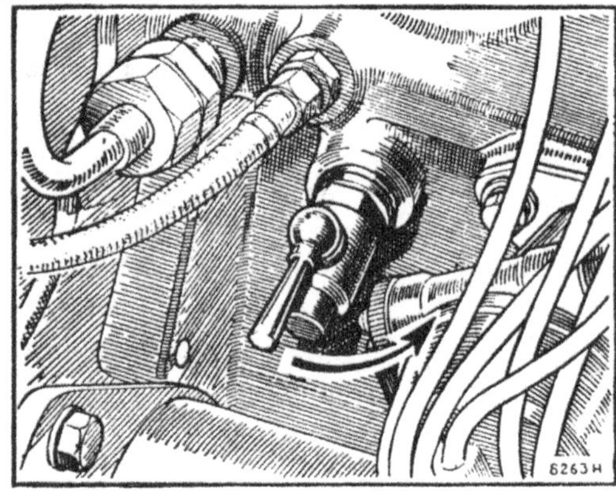

The cylinder block drain tap is on the right-hand side of the block at the rear. Turn in the direction of the arrow to open

Frost precautions

Water, when it freezes, expands, and if precautions are not taken there is considerable risk of bursting the radiator, cylinder block, or heater (where fitted). Such damage may be avoided by draining the cooling system when the vehicle is left for any length of time in frosty weather, or by adding anti-freeze to the water.

Warning

When a heater unit is fitted an anti-freeze solution must be added in the cooling system since no provision is made for draining the heater.

Do not use radiator anti-freeze solution in the windscreen-washing equipment (where fitted).

Anti-freeze solutions

Anti-freeze can remain in the cooling system for two years provided that the specific gravity of the coolant is checked periodically and anti-freeze added as necessary. This operation should be carried out by an authorized Distributor or Dealer.

After the second winter the system should be drained and refilled with fresh water, and the appropriate amount of anti-freeze added when required.

Only anti-freeze of the ethylene glycol or glycerine type is suitable for use in the cooling system. We recommend owners to use Bluecol Anti-freeze (non-corrosive) in order to protect the cooling system during frosty weather and reduce corrosion to a minimum. We also approve the use of any anti-freeze which conforms to Specification B.S.3151 or B.S.3152.

The correct quantities of anti-freeze for different degrees of frost protection are:

Anti-freeze	*Commences to freeze*		*Frozen solid*		*Amount of anti-freeze*		
%	° C.	° F.	° C.	° F.	Pts.	U.S. Pts.	Litres
25	—13	9	—26	—15	2½	3	1·4
33⅓	—19	—2	—36	—33	3½	4	2·0
50	—36	—33	—48	—53	5	6	2·8

Before adding anti-freeze mixture to the radiator it is advisable to clean out the cooling system thoroughly by flushing out the passages with a hose inserted in the filler cap while keeping the drain taps open.

Only top up when the cooling system is at its normal running temperature, in order to avoid losing anti-freeze due to expansion.

Make sure that the cooling system is water-tight, examine all joints, and replace any defective rubber hose with new.

Draining the cooling system

There are two drain taps provided, one on the radiator bottom tank and the other on the right-hand side of the cylinder block. To drain the coolant stand the car on level ground and open both taps.

When draining in freezing weather, do so when the engine is hot. Run the engine slowly for one minute when the water has ceased flowing to clear any water from the pump and other places where it might collect. Finally, leave a reminder on the vehicle to the effect that the cooling system has been drained.

If the system contains anti-freeze remember to collect it in a clean container for future use.

Filling the cooling system

To avoid wastage by overflow add just sufficient coolant to cover the bottom of the header tank. Run the engine until it is hot and add sufficient coolant to bring the surface to the level of the indicator positioned inside the header tank below the filler neck.

NOTE.—If a heater is fitted ensure that the heater temperature control is set to 'HOT' when draining or filling the system.

IGNITION

Static ignition timing

The point where ignition should start is given in **'GENERAL DATA'**. With the crankshaft stationary at this position, the contact breaker points should be just beginning to open. When the engine is running timing is varied by a centrifugal advance mechanism and a vacuum control.

Checking static ignition timing

The information given below describes a method of checking the ignition timing; it does not detail the resetting of the timing when the distributor has been removed from the engine.

Check that the contact points are set to the correct gap when on the peak of the distributor cam (see page 32).

The rim of the crankshaft pulley has a small groove which will correspond with the long pointer on the timing cover when Nos. 1 and 4 pistons are at T.D.C.; the other two pointers indicate 5° and 10° B.T.D.C. To turn the pulley

(Right) The distributor adjusting nut (arrowed). (Left) The timing cover pointers and crankshaft pulley groove

to the required position remove the sparking plugs, engage top gear, and push the car forward until the groove in the pulley is in the correct position (see **'GENERAL DATA'**).

With the crankshaft in this position the contact points should be just about to open. If the points are open, turn the knurled nut towards 'R' until they are closed; if they are closed, turn the nut towards 'A'. In both cases turn the nut until the points are just parting.

A simple electrical method may be used to ensure an accurate check. Connect a 12-volt bulb between the low-tension terminal on the side of the distributor and a good earth point on the engine. Switch on the ignition. If the bulb lights, turn the knurled nut towards 'R' until the light goes out and then back towards 'A' until it just lights. This will give the correct static timing.

If pinking should occur due to the use of a fuel of a lower range than our recommendations, retarding the ignition 2 to 3° can be tolerated. In no circumstances should the ignition be advanced beyond the correct setting.

If this adjustment cannot be made with the knurled nut, consult your Distributor/Dealer.

Distributor (lubrication)

Cam bearing

Remove the rotor arm from the top of the distributor drive spindle and add a few drops of oil Ref. E (page 72) to the cam bearing. Do not remove the screw that is exposed to view; there is a clearance between the screw and the inner face of the cam spindle for the oil to pass. Replace the rotor arm with its drive lug correctly engaging the spindle slot and push it onto the spindle as far as it will go.

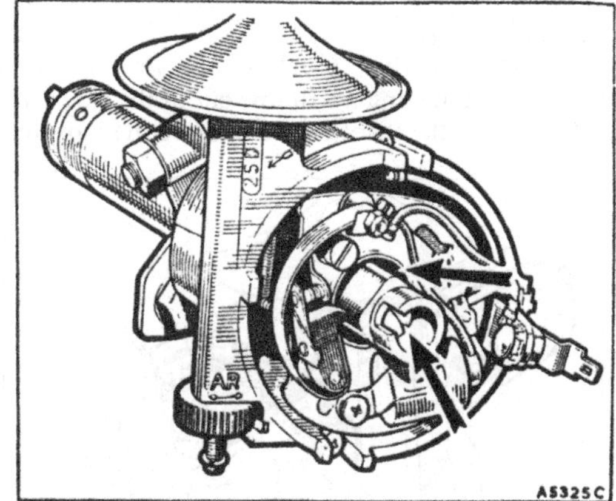

The distributor cam bearing and automatic timing control lubricating points

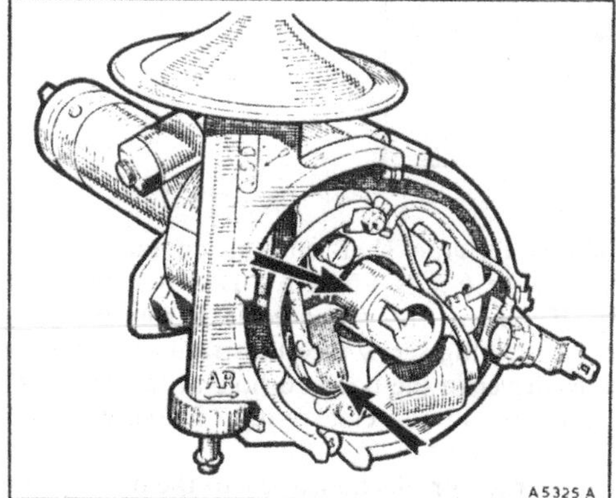

The distributor cam spindle and contact breaker lubricating points

Cam spindle and contact breaker pivot

Smear a very small amount of grease to Ref. C (page 72) on the cam spindle and also on the contact breaker pivot. Do not allow the grease to get on the contacts; lubricate sparingly.

Automatic advance control

Add a few drops of oil to Ref. E (page 72) through the hole in the contact breaker base plate to lubricate the automatic advance mechanism. Do not over-oil or allow any oil to get on or near the contacts. Carefully wipe away any surplus oil and see that the contact breaker points are clean.

IGNITION

Distributor (mechanical check)

Check the functioning of the automatic advance and retard mechanism as follows.

Centrifugal advance mechanism

Remove the distributor cap and grasp the rotor firmly. Turn the rotor arm in the direction of rotation and release it. The rotor arm should return to its original position without showing any tendency to stick.

Vacuum advance

Use a screwdriver to check the movement of the moving plate. Where a modified cap having a window cut in the side is available fit the cap and start the engine. Open the throttle and observe the movement of the contact breaker plate.

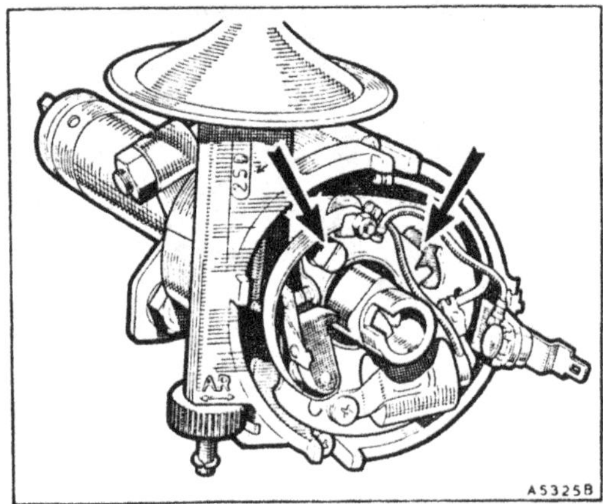

The distributor points, contact plate securing screws, and the (screwdriver) adjusting slot, indicated by arrows

Contact breaker

Remove the distributor cap and turn the crankshaft until the contacts are fully open. Check the gap with a feeler gauge (see 'GENERAL DATA'); the gauge should be a sliding fit in the gap. If the gap varies appreciably from the gauge thickness, slacken the contact plate securing screw (see illustration) and adjust the contact gap by inserting a screwdriver in the notched hole at the end of the plate and turning clockwise to decrease and anti-clockwise to increase the gap. Retighten the securing screw.

If the contact breaker points are burned or blackened, clean them with a fine carborundum stone or with fine emery-cloth.

Cleaning the contacts is made easier if the contact breaker lever carrying the moving contact is removed. To do this unscrew the nut securing the end of the spring, remove the spring washer, flat washer, and both lead terminals, and lift off the lever complete with spring. After cleaning refit the contact breaker and check the gap.

The high-tension cables connecting the distributor to the sparking plugs may, after long use, also show signs of perishing. They must then be replaced by the correct type of ignition cable. Cut the cables to length, fill the holes in the cap with silicone grease, push the cables well home in the cap, and secure with the pointed screws.

Sparking plugs

Remove the plugs and clean off all carbon deposit from the electrodes and plug threads with a stiff brush dipped in paraffin (kerosene).

Check the plug gaps, and reset if necessary to the recommended clearance (see 'GENERAL DATA'). When resetting, bend the side electrode only—never bend the centre electrode as this may split the insulator tip.

When refitting the plugs, make sure that the copper washers are not defective in any way. If they have become worn and flattened, fit new ones to ensure a gastight joint. Screw the plug down by hand as far as possible, then use a spanner for tightening only. Always use a tubular box spanner to avoid possible damage to the insulator, and do not under any circumstances use a movable wrench. Never overtighten a plug, but ensure that a good joint is made between the plug body, washer, and cylinder head.

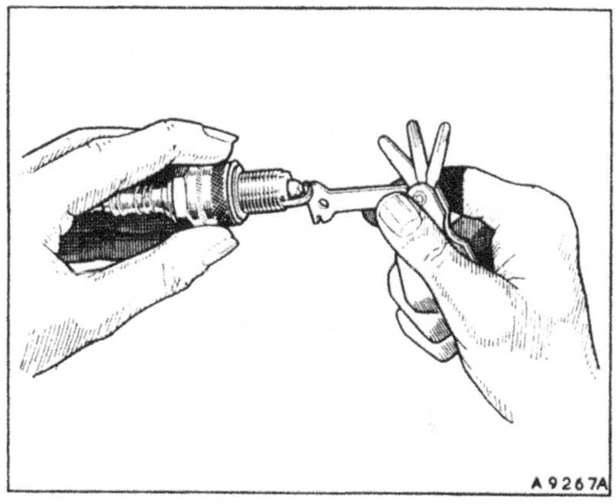

Use a Champion sparking plug gauge and setting tool. Move the side and never the centre electrode

The correct grade of sparking plug for use under normal driving conditions is the Champion N–9Y. Plugs of a lower heat range (hotter running) should not be used, otherwise pre-ignition will occur, with consequent rise in combustion temperature and resulting engine damage. For competition work or hard driving where high output is consistently sustained the Champion N3 sparking plug should be used. This is a cooler-running plug and will ensure lower combustion temperatures and an increased margin of safety. Accumulated deposits of carbon, leaking or cracked insulators, and thin electrodes are all causes of pre-ignition. The plugs should therefore be examined, cleaned, and adjusted at the specified intervals and defective ones renewed.

Coil

The coil requires no attention beyond keeping its exterior clean, particularly between the terminals, and occasionally checking that the terminal connections are quite tight.

If the high-tension cable needs renewal it must be replaced by the correct type. Bare the end of the cable for $\frac{1}{4}$ in. (6 mm.), pass it through its moulded terminal and washer, and spread out the strands to ensure good contact.

ELECTRICAL

Batteries

The batteries are located in trays beneath the rear floor panel. To gain access to them remove the moulded carpet, release the five screws in the floor panel, and remove the panel.

The battery electrolyte must be maintained at the correct level.

Remove the filler plugs weekly and examine the level of the electrolyte in each cell. If necessary, add sufficient distilled water until the perforated separator guard in each cell is just covered. Do not overfill. More frequent topping up may be necessary in hot climates or if long daily runs are made.

Do not use tap-water and do not use a naked light when examining the condition of the cells. Wipe away all dirt and moisture from the top of the battery.

Checking the specific gravity

Check the condition of the battery by taking hydrometer readings of the specific gravity of the electrolyte in each of the cells. Readings should not be

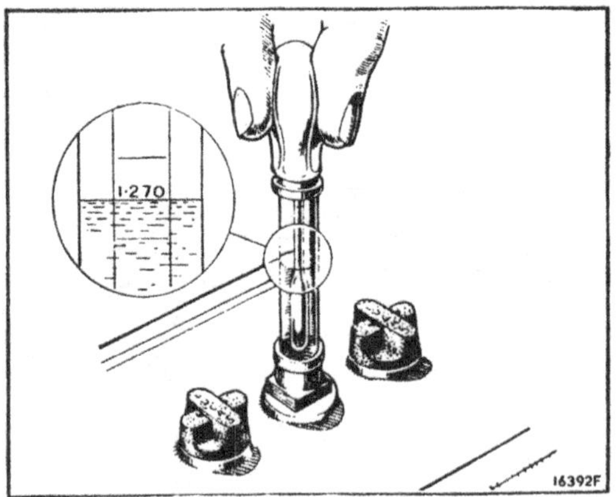

Taking hydrometer readings

taken immediately after topping up the cells. The hydrometer must be held vertically and the readings taken at eye-level. Check that the float is free and take care not to draw in too much electrolyte. The specific gravity readings and their indications are as follows:

	For climates below 27° C. (80° F.)	For climates above 27° C. (80° F.)
Battery fully charged	1·270 to 1·290	1·210 to 1·230
Battery about half-charged	1·190 to 1·210	1·130 to 1·150
Battery fully discharged	1·110 to 1·130	1·050 to 1·070

These figures are given assuming that the temperature of the solution is about 16° C. (60° F.). If the temperature of the electrolyte exceeds 16° C. (60° F.) ·002 must be added to the hydrometer reading for each 3° C. (5° F.) rise to give the true specific gravity. Similarly, ·002 must be subtracted from the hydrometer reading for every 3° C. (5° F.) below 16° C. (60° F.). The readings for all cells should be approximately the same. If one cell gives a reading very different from the rest the battery should be examined by an authorized Distributor or Dealer.

Never leave the battery in a discharged condition for any length of time. Have it fully charged, and every fortnight give it a short refreshing charge to prevent any tendency for the plates to become permanently sulphated.

Fuel pump

The fuel pump is mounted on a bracket secured to the heelboard adjacent to the front of the right-hand rear spring.

Windscreen wiper

To reposition a wiper arm on the spindle, the arm can be withdrawn when the small spring clip is held clear of the retaining groove. **Replace the arm in the required position and push it hard down onto the spindle until it is secured in position by the retaining clip.**

To remove a wiper blade rubber, withdraw the retaining rubber stop from one end of the wiper blade and slide the rubber from the retaining clips.

To ensure efficient wiping it is recommended that the blade rubbers are renewed annually.

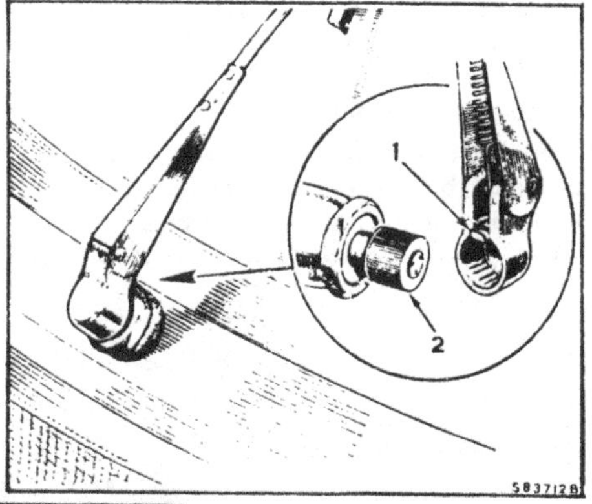

Windscreen wiper arm

1. Retaining clip.
2. Splined spindle.

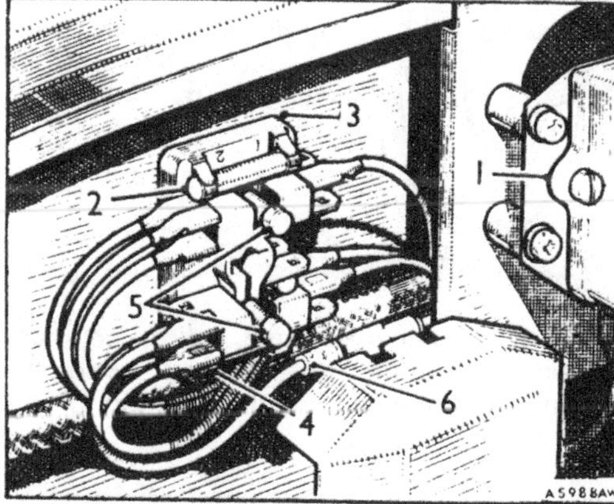

Regulator and fuse block

1. Regulator.
2. AUX. IGN. fuse (35-amp.).
3. Fuse block.
4. AUX. fuse (35-amp.).
5. Spare fuses.
6. Line fuse — heated backlight (when fitted).

Fuses

The fuses are housed in a separate fuse block on the engine bulkhead.

The fuse connecting terminals 'A1' and 'A2' protects the accessories that operate irrespective of whether the ignition is on or off.

The fuse connecting terminals 'A3' and 'A4' protects the accessories that operate only when the ignition is switched on (stop lights, direction indicators, etc.).

ELECTRICAL

Blown fuses

The units which are protected by the fuses can readily be identified on the wiring diagram. A blown fuse is indicated by the failure of all the units protected by it, and is confirmed by examination of the fuse when withdrawn.

Before renewing a blown fuse inspect the wiring of the units that have failed for evidence of a short circuit or other fault.

Spare fuses are provided and it is important to use only the correct replacement fuse. The fusing value is marked on a coloured paper slip inside the glass tube of the fuse.

Voltage regulator

This is a sealed unit located on the right-hand front wheel arch which controls the charging rate of the dynamo in accordance with the needs of the batteries. It requires no attention and should not be disturbed.

Jammed starter pinion

If the starter pinion becomes jammed in mesh with the flywheel, it can usually be freed by turning the starter armature with a spanner applied to the shaft extension at the commutator end.

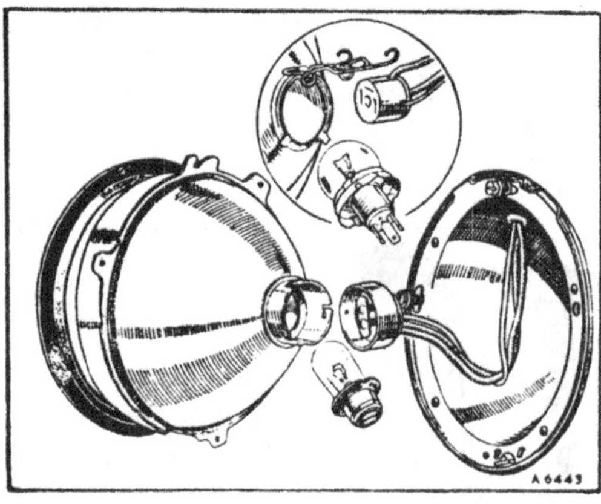

The headlamp light unit (L.H.D. except Europe and North America) removed showing the bulb holder and back-shell, etc., with the European-type lamp inset

Headlamps (European type)

To change a bulb ease the rim off the bottom of the lamp, pull the bottom of the rim forward and lift off the retaining lugs at the top of the lamp. Remove the three inner rim retaining screws, remove the rim and pull the light unit forward from the back-shell.

Early Tourer cars: Press the light unit and turn anti-clockwise to release it from the back-shell.

The bulb is released by withdrawing the three-pin socket and pinching the two ends of the wire retaining clip to clear the bulb flange. When replacing the bulb care must be taken to see that the rectangular pip on the bulb flange engages the slot in the reflector seating. Replace the spring clip with its coils resting in the base of the bulb flange and engaging the two retaining lugs on the reflector seating for the bulb.

Headlights (L.H.D. except Europe and North America)

Access to the bulb is obtained in the same manner as that described for European-type headlamps. Twist the back-shell anti-clockwise and pull it off. The bulb can then be withdrawn from its holder.

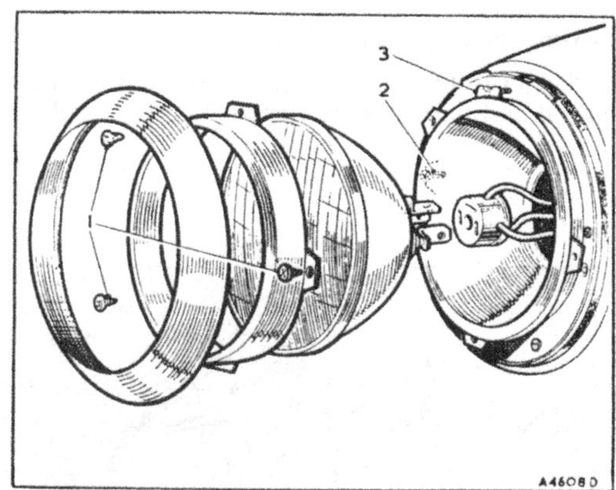

The U.K. sealed-beam headlamp, showing:

1. Retaining plate screws.
2. Horizontal adjustment screw.
3. Vertical adjustment screw.

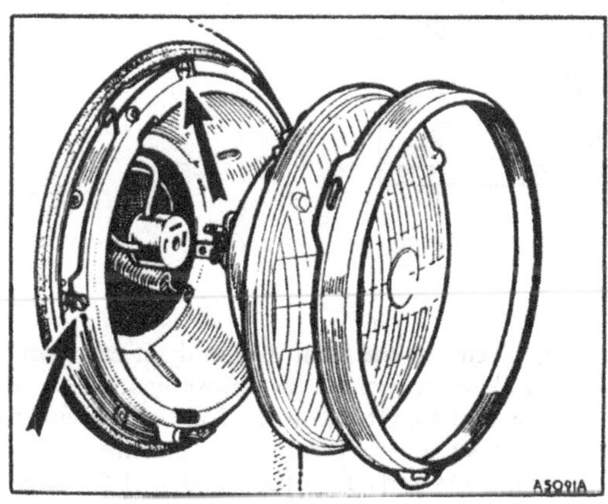

The North American sealedbeam headlamp with the beam adjusting screws indicated by the arrows

Headlamps (U.K. sealed-beam type)

To change a sealed-beam light unit ease the outer rim off the bottom of the lamp, pull the bottom of the rim forward and lift off the retaining lugs at the top of the lamp.

Remove the three inner rim retaining screws and remove the rim. Pull the light unit from the back-shell and disconnect the three-pin plug to release it from the back-shell.

ELECTRICAL

Headlamps (North American sealed-beam type)

To change a sealed-beam light unit, lift the bottom of the outer rim forwards and upwards, and detach the rim. Slacken the three Phillips screws securing the light unit retaining rim and turn the rim anti-clockwise to remove, supporting the lens of the light unit at the same time. Pull off the three-pin plug from the rear of the light unit.

Setting the headlight beams

The headlight beams must be set so that the main driving beams are straight ahead and parallel with the road surface and with each other, or in accordance

*The side and direction indi-
cator lamp*

with the local regulations. To adjust, remove the lamp rim and set each lamp to the correct position in the vertical plane by turning the adjusting screw at the top of the light unit in a clockwise direction to raise and anti-clockwise to lower the beam. Horizontal adjustment is made by turning the adjustment screw on the right-hand side of the light unit. On early European and L.H.D. except Europe and North American type units two horizontal adjusting screws are fitted.

Checking and resetting should be carried out at the beginning of each winter. This work is best entrusted to a Distributor/Dealer, who will have specialist equipment available for this purpose.

Side and direction indicator lamps

Extract the two retaining screws to release the plated rim and the lens to gain access to both the light and direction indicator bulbs.

Stop and tail and direction indicator lamps

Extract the one retaining screw from the bottom of the lamp and slide the lens upwards to release it from the retaining tongue at the top of the lamp.

Panel and warning lights

The panel and warning light bulb holders are a push fit in their housings and are accessible from below the fascia panel.

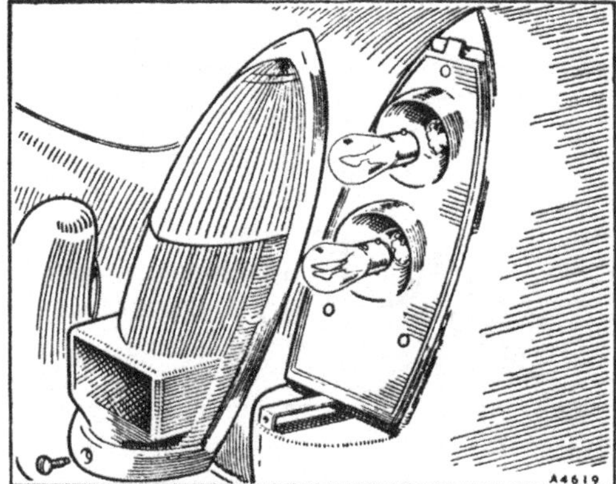

The stop/tail and flashing indicator lights

The number-plate lamps

Number-plate lamps

The rear number-plate lamps are fitted one to each inside face of the rear bumper over-riders.

To gain access to a lamp bulb remove the two securing screws and retain the nuts and distance pieces from the inside of the over-rider. Take off the lamp hood and remove the bulb.

When refitting, ensure that the wedge-shaped distance piece is fitted with its thickest edge towards the rear.

ELECTRICAL

Reverse lamps

To renew a lamp bulb, remove the two securing screws and withdraw the lens. Press the bulb down towards the lower contact and withdraw it from the lamp.

Fit one end of the new bulb into the hole in the lower contact then press the top of the bulb until the point on the cap engages in the hole in the upper contact.

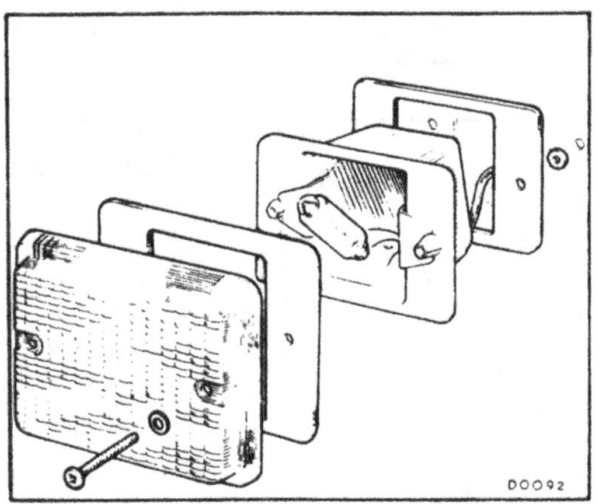

The reverse lamp

Dynamo bearing

Add two or three drops of engine oil to Ref. E (page 72) to the dynamo bearing through the central hole in the rear end bearing plate. Do not over-oil.

Replacement bulbs	Volts	Watts	BMC Part No.
Headlamp, L.H.D. (except North America and Europe)	12	50/40	BFS 415
Headlamps (Europe except France)	12	45/40	BFS 410
Headlamp (France only)	12	45/40	BFS 411
Sidelamp	12	6	BFS 989
Direction indicator, front	12	21	BFS 382
Direction indicator, rear	12	21	BFS 382
Stop and tail lamps	12	6/21	BFS 380
Number-plate illumination lamp	12	6	BFS 207
Panel and warning lights	12	2·2	BFS 987
Reverse lamp	12	21	27H 8814

WIRING DIAGRAM

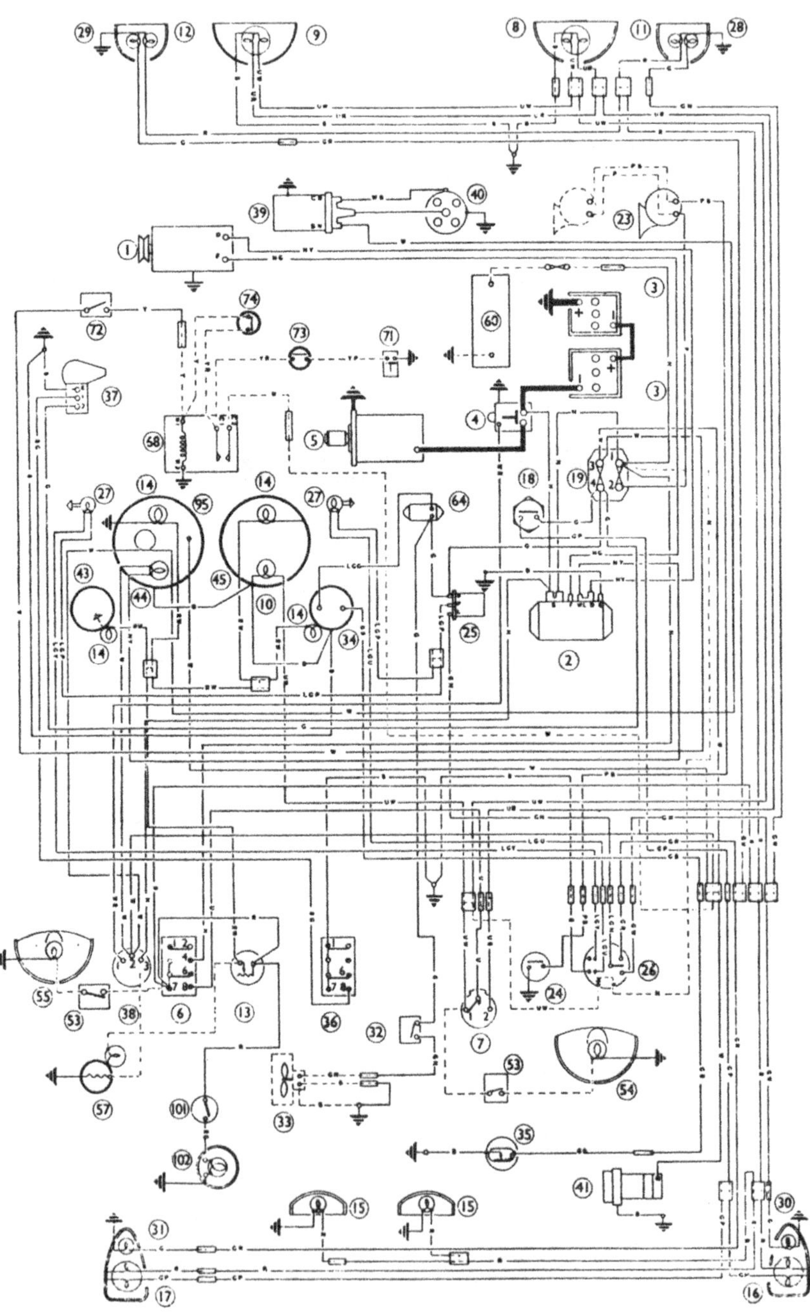

KEY TO WIRING DIAGRAM

1. Dynamo.
2. Control box.
3. Battery—6-volt.
4. Starter solenoid.
5. Starter motor.
6. Lighting switch.
7. Headlight dip switch.
8. R.H. headlamp.
9. L.H. headlamp.
10. Main-beam warning light.
11. R.H. side lamp.
12. L.H. side lamp.
13. Rheostat—panel lights.
14. Panel lights.
15. Number-plate lamps.
16. R.H. stop/tail lamp.
17. L.H. stop/tail lamp.
18. Stop light switch.
19. Fuse unit.
23. Horn (twin when fitted*).
24. Horn-push.
25. Flasher unit.
26. Direction indicator (and headlight flasher*) switch.
27. Direction indicator warning lights.
28. R.H. front flasher lamp.
29. L.H. front flasher lamp.
30. R.H. rear flasher lamp.
31. L.H. rear flasher lamp.
32. Heater or fresh-air motor switch.
33. Heater or fresh-air motor.*
34. Fuel gauge.
35. Fuel gauge tank unit.
36. Windscreen wiper switch.
37. Windscreen wiper motor.
38. Ignition/starter switch.
39. Ignition coil.
40. Distributor.
41. Fuel pump.
43. Oil pressure gauge.
44. Ignition warning lamp.
45. Speedometer.
53. Fog or driving light switch.*
54. Driving lamp.*
55. Fog lamp.*
57. Cigar-lighter—illuminated.*
60. Radio.*
63. Flasher relay.
64. Bi-metal instrument voltage stabillzer.
68. Overdrive relay unit.*
71. Overdrive solenoid.*
72. Overdrive manual control switch.*
73. Overdrive gear switch.*
74. Overdrive throttle switch.*
95. Tachometer.
101. Map light switch.
102. Map light.

CABLE COLOUR CODE

N.	Brown.	P.	Purple.	W.	White.
U.	Blue.	G.	Green.	Y.	Yellow.
R.	Red.	L.G.	Light Green.	B.	Black.

When a cable has two colour code letters the first denotes the main colour and the second denotes the tracer colour.

Items marked thus * may be fitted as an optional extra.

ENGINE/TRANSMISSION

Checking engine oil level (A)

The level of the oil in the engine sump is indicated by the dipstick on the right-hand side of the engine. Maintain the level at the 'MAX' mark on the dipstick and never allow it to fall below the 'MIN' mark.

The filler is on the forward end of the rocker cover and is provided with a quick-action cap. The filler cap also incorporates a filter for the closed-circuit crankcase breathing intake (later cars).

The oil level should always be checked before a long run.

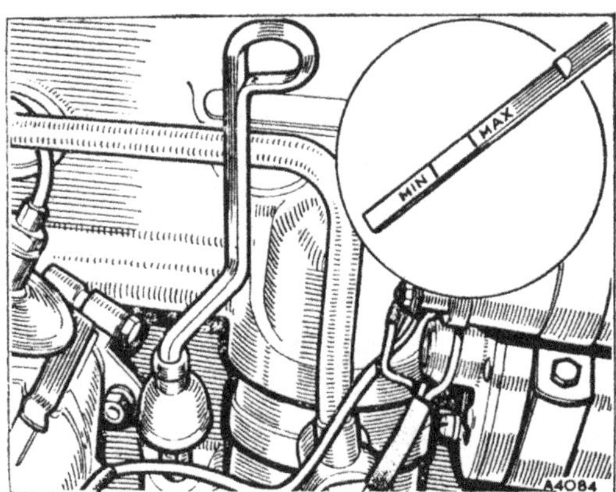

The engine oil dipstick with the markings shown in the inset

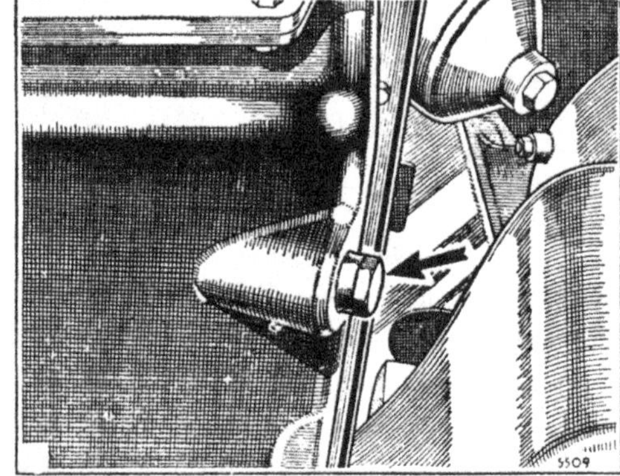

The engine sump drain plug is located on the right-hand side of the pump

Draining the sump (A)

Drain the oil from the engine sump and refill with new oil. The drain plug is on the right-hand side of the sump and should be removed after a journey while the oil is still warm and will drain easily.

The sump capacity is shown in 'GENERAL DATA'.

Oil filter

The external oil filter is of the renewable-element type and is located on the right-hand side of the cylinder block. The filter is released by undoing the central bolt securing the filter body to the filter head. Wash out the casing with petrol (gasoline) and dry it before fitting a new felt-type element. Ensure that the filter head to casing sealing ring is correctly positioned, clean, and serviceable. Hold the casing against spring pressure before finally tightening the central fixing bolt and ascertain that the casing is seating centrally on the seal.

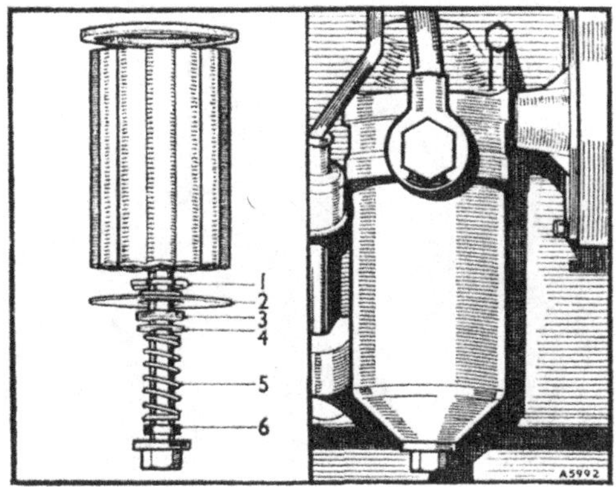

The engine oil filter, showing the positions in which the washers are fitted below the element

1. Retaining clip.
2. Element pressure plate.
3. Felt washer.
4. Steel washer.
5. Pressure spring.
6. Rubber washer.

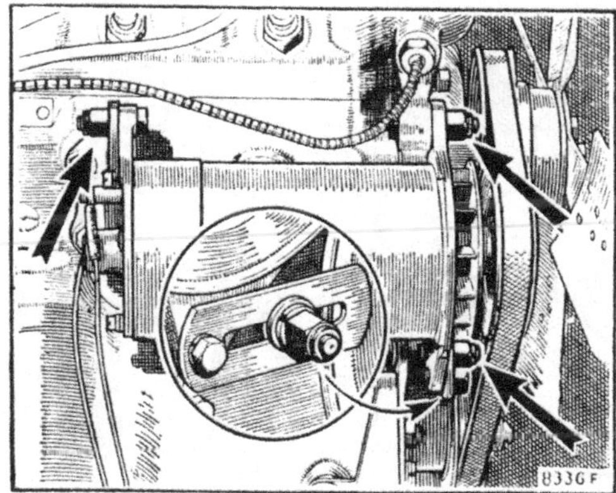

The four dynamo securing bolts, all of which must be slackened for belt adjustment

Dynamo driving belt

To adjust the belt tension slacken the four dynamo-securing bolts and move the dynamo the required amount by hand. Care should be taken to avoid overtightening the belt. Tighten up the bolts thoroughly, particularly the one passing through the slotted adjusting link.

ENGINE/TRANSMISSION

Water pump (C)

Remove the plug on the water pump casing and lubricate sparingly with grease.

Valve rockers

Remove the valve rocker cover and test the clearance between the rocker arms and the valve stems by inserting a ·015 in. (·38 mm.) feeler gauge between them. The blade should be a sliding fit when the valves are tested in the following order while the engine is cold:

The water pump lubrication plug

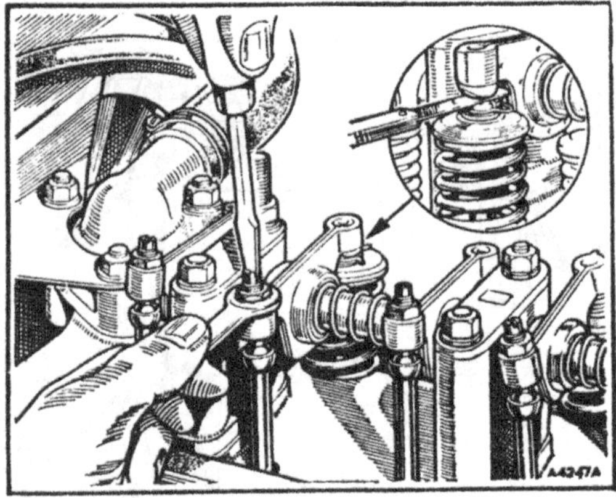

The method of setting the valve clearance, and (inset) using a feeler gauge to check the clearance

Test No. 1 valve with No. 8 fully open.   Test No. 8 valve with No. 1 fully open.

„	„	3	„	„	„	6	„	„		„	„	6	„	„	„	3	„	„
„	„	5	„	„	„	4	„	„		„	„	4	„	„	„	5	„	„
„	„	2	„	„	„	7	„	„		„	„	7	„	„	„	2	„	„

To adjust the clearance slacken the adjusting screw locknut on the opposite end of the rocker arm and rotate the screw clockwise to reduce the clearance or anti-clockwise to increase it. Retighten the locknut when the clearance is correct, holding the screw against rotation with a screwdriver.

Closed-circuit breathing

An air filter is incorporated in the oil filler cap. The cap is serviced only as a complete assembly.

To test the control valve, run the engine at idling speed while at normal running temperature. Remove the oil filler cap. If the valve is functioning correctly the engine speed will rise by approximately 200 r.p.m. as the cap is removed, the change being audibly noticeable. If no change in speed occurs, service the valve as follows:

Remove the spring clip and dismantle the valve. Clean all metal parts with a solvent (trichlorethylene, fuel, etc.). **Do not use an abrasive.** If deposits are difficult to remove immerse in boiling water before applying the solvent. Clean the diaphragm with detergent or methylated spirits.

Reassemble the valve, making sure that the metering needle is in the cruciform guides and the diaphragm is seated correctly.

NOTE—The first-type valve assembly (without the cruciform guides) is serviced only as an assembly.

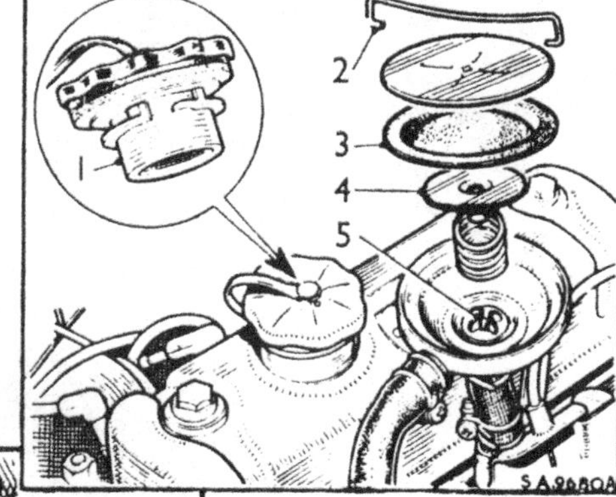

The breather control valve (second type) and combined air filter/oil filler cap

1. Filler cap.
2. Spring clip.
3. Diaphragm.
4. Metering valve.
5. Cruciform guides.

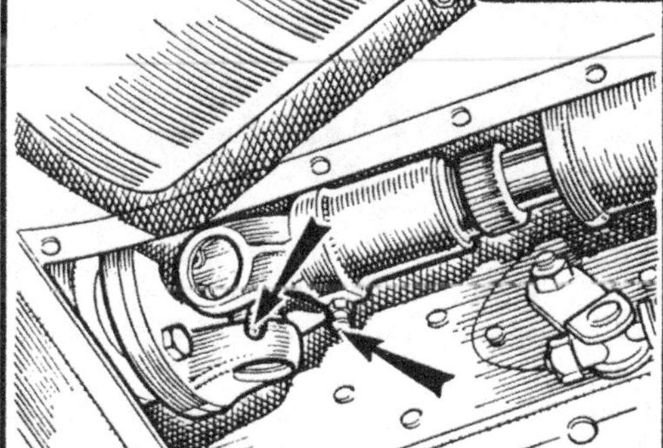

The lubrication nipples for the front universal joint (early Tourer cars) and the sliding yoke

Propeller shaft

Lubrication nipples are provided on the front and rear universal joints (early Tourer cars) and on the sliding yoke at the front end of the propeller shaft. To lubricate, give three or four strokes of the grease gun filled to Ref. C (page 72).

ENGINE/TRANSMISSION

Gearbox and overdrive

When topping up or refilling ensure that the level does not rise above the 'HIGH' mark on the dipstick.

The combined filler plug and dipstick for the gearbox is located beneath the rubber plug on the tunnel behind the speaker panel.

When the overdrive is fitted, remove the overdrive drain plug and the gearbox drain plug and drain off the oil. Remove the overdrive filter cover plate and gasket from the left-hand side of the unit, and withdraw the filter gauze seal and magnetic rings. Clean, replace, and refill the gearbox with oil to Ref. A (page 72).

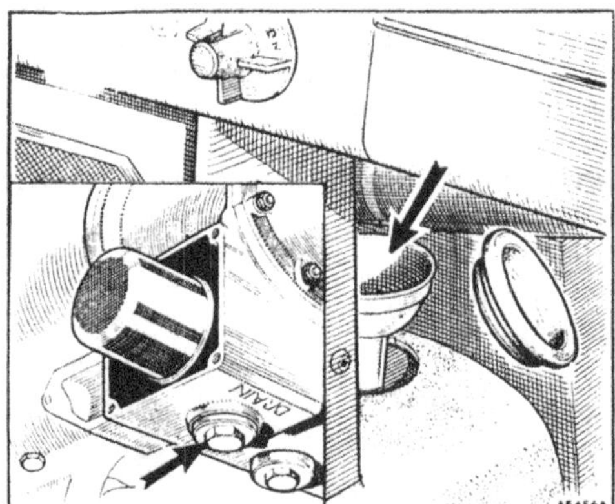

The gearbox oil filler plug and (arrowed) a funnel passing through the tunnel to the gearbox. The overdrive filter is shown inset

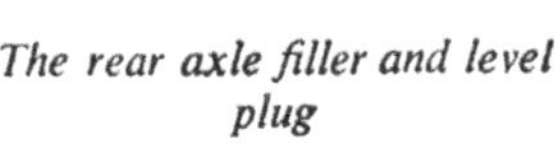

The rear axle filler and level plug

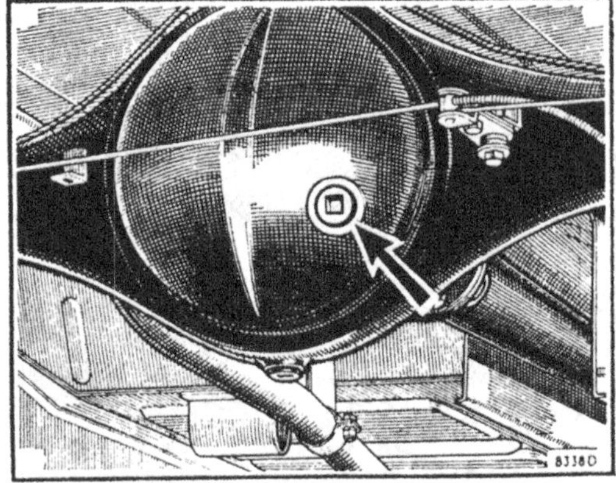

Rear axle

A combined oil filler and level plug is located on the rear of the axle. The oil level should be maintained at the bottom of the plug aperture. Ensure that the car is standing level when checking.

After topping up the oil level allow sufficient time for any surplus oil, which may have been added accidentally, to run out of the aperture before replacing the plug. On no account must the axle be overfilled.

NOTE.—It is essential that only Hypoid oil be used in the rear axle.

CARBURETTERS

Slow-running adjustment and synchronization

When the engine is fully run in the slow running may require adjustment. This must only be carried out when the engine has reached its normal running temperature.

As the needle size is determined during engine development, tuning of the carburetters is confined to correct idling setting. Slacken the actuating arms on the throttle spindle interconnection. Close both throttles fully by unscrewing the throttle adjusting screws, then open each throttle by screwing down each screw one turn.

Remove the suction chamber and piston assemblies, marking each to ensure replacement in their original positions, remove air cleaners and disconnect the mixture control cable. Screw the jet adjusting nuts until each jet is flush with the bridge of its carburetter, or as near to this as possible (both jets being in the same relative position to the bridge of their respective carburetters). Replace the

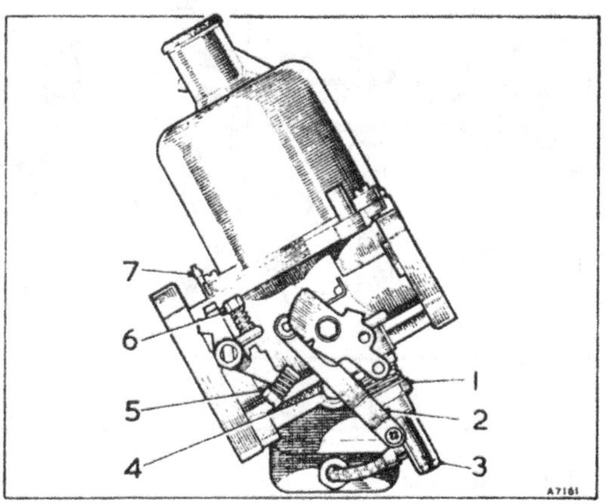

The carburetter showing:

1. Jet adjusting nut.
2. Jet link.
3. Jet head.
4. Float-chamber securing nut.
5. Fast idling adjusting screw.
6. Throttle adjusting screw.
7. Vacuum ignition take-off.

pistons and suction chamber assemblies, and check that the pistons fall freely onto the bridge of the carburetters (by means of the piston lifting pins). Turn down each jet adjusting nut two complete turns (12 flats).

Restart the engine, and turn the throttle adjusting screws to give the desired idling speed by moving each screw an equal amount. By listening to the hiss in the intakes, adjust the throttle adjusting screws until the intensity of the hiss is similar on both intakes. This will synchronize the throttles.

When this is satisfactory, the mixture should be adjusted by screwing each jet adjusting nut, up to weaken, or down to enrich, by the same amount until the fastest idling speed consistent with even firing is obtained. During this adjustment it is necessary to press the jets upwards and ensure that they are in contact with the adjusting nuts.

As the mixture is adjusted the engine will probably run faster and it may therefore be necessary to unscrew the throttle adjusting screws a little, each by the same amount, to reduce the speed.

CARBURETTERS

Now check the mixture strength by lifting the piston of the front carburetter by approximately $\frac{1}{32}$ in. (·75 mm.) when:

   (1) If the engine speed increases, the mixture strength of the front carburetter is too rich.

   (2) If the engine speed immediately decreases, the mixture strength of the front carburetter is too weak.

   (3) If the engine speed momentarily increases very slightly, the mixture strength of the front carburetter is correct.

Repeat the operation at the rear carburetter, and after adjustment re-check the front carburetter, since both carburetters are interdependent.

When the mixture is correct the exhaust note should be regular and even. If it is irregular, with a splashy type of misfire and colourless exhaust, the mixture is too weak. If there is a regular or rhythmical type of misfire in the exhaust beat, together with a blackish exhaust, then the mixture is too rich.

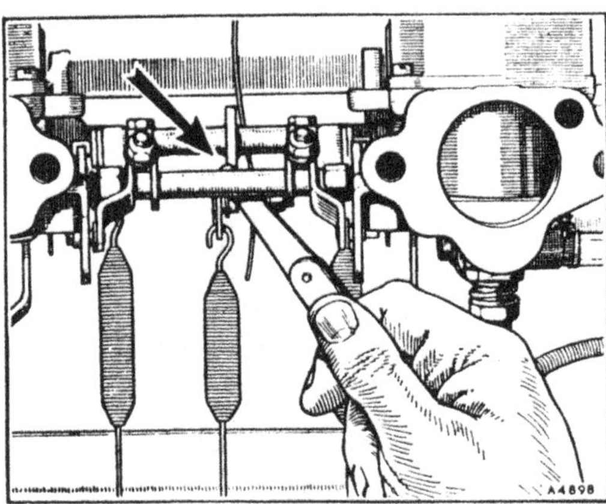

The feeler between the throttle shaft stop and the choke interconnecting rod

Throttle linkage

Each throttle is operated by a lever and pin, with the pin working in a forked lever attached to the throttle spindle. A clearance exists between the pin and fork which must be maintained when the throttle is closed and the engine idling to prevent any load from the accelerator linkage being transferred to the throttle butterfly and spindle.

To set this clearance, with the throttle shaft levers free on the throttle shaft, put a ·012 in. (·305 mm.) feeler between the throttle shaft stop and the mixture (choke) control interconnecting rod. Move the throttle shaft lever downwards until the lever pin rests lightly on the lower arm of the fork in the carburetter throttle lever. Tighten the clamp bolt of the throttle shaft lever at this position. When both carburetters have been dealt with, remove the feeler. The pins on the throttle shaft should then have clearance in the forks.

Reconnect the mixture control cable, ensuring that the jet heads return against the lower face of the jet adjusting nuts when the mixture control is pushed fully in. Pull out the mixture control knob on the dash panel until the linkage is about to move the carburetter jets a minimum of $\frac{1}{4}$ in. (6 mm.) and adjust the fast-idle adjusting screws to give an engine speed of about 1,000 r.p.m. when hot.

Carburetter lubrication

The damper reservoir on each carburetter must be topped up periodically with thin engine oil to Ref. E (page 72). Under no circumstances should a heavy-bodied lubricant be used. Unscrew the damper cap, withdraw the damper, and top up the reservoir until the oil level is $\frac{1}{2}$ in. (13 mm.) above the top of the hollow piston rod. Push the damper assembly back into position and screw the cap firmly into the reservoir.

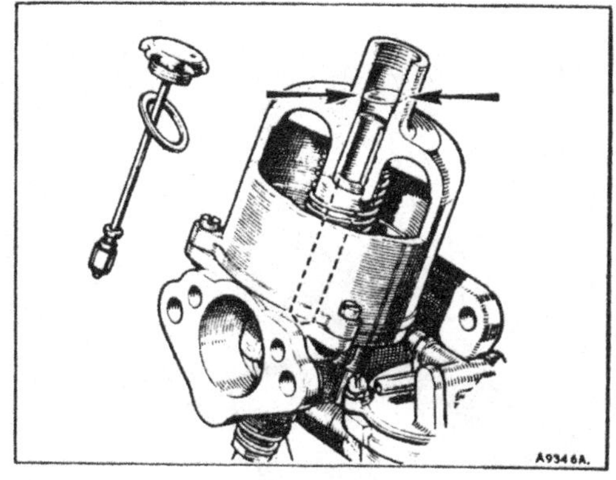

Lubricating the carburetter piston dampers

Air cleaner (dry type)

To renew the air filter element unscrew the bolts securing each air cleaner to the choke bracket and fixing plate respectively and remove from the car.

Remove the base plate and withdraw the paper element. Clean the inside of the casing thoroughly and reassemble, using a new element.

BRAKES

Rear brake linings

To inspect the rear brake linings block the front wheels, and release the hand brake.

Remove the road wheel (see page 61), slacken off the brake-shoe adjuster fully and withdraw the brake-drum.

Inspect the linings for wear and blow out the backplate assembly and drum. Replace the drum and road wheel and adjust the brake-shoes.

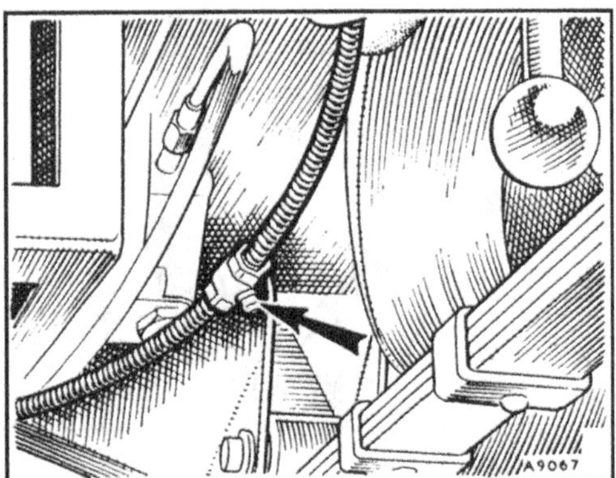

A grease nipple is provided on the hand brake cable and will be found near the front end of the right-hand rear spring

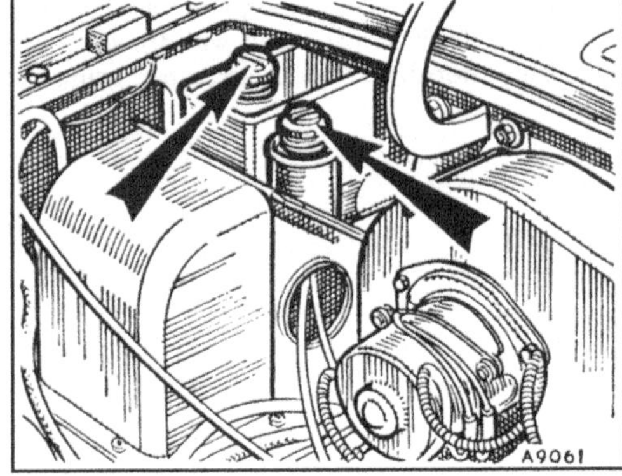

The level of the fluid in the hydraulic brake and clutch master cylinders should be maintained at ½ in. (13 mm.) below the bottom of the filler cap

Hand brake cable

A lubrication nipple is provided on the hand brake cable. To lubricate charge the nipple with grease to Ref. C (page 72).

Brake and clutch master cylinder

To check the fluid level in the hydraulic brake and clutch master cylinders remove the filler caps (see illustration above). When topping up use only Lockheed Disc Brake Fluid (Series II).

Disc brakes

Examine the disc brake friction pads for wear. Wear on the pads is automatically compensated for during braking operations and manual adjustment is not therefore required. If the wear on one pad is greater than on the other their operating positions should be changed over.

When the pads have worn to a minimum thickness of $\frac{1}{16}$ in. (1·6 mm.) they must be renewed.

Entrust this work to an authorized Distributor or Dealer.

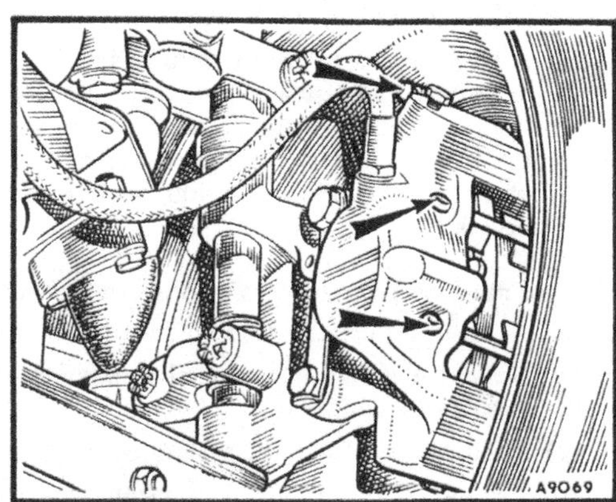

The upper arrow indicates the bleed nipple and the lower arrows the spring clip retaining pins

The rear brake-shoes are adjusted by a square-headed adjuster behind the brake backplate

Rear brake adjustment

Excessive brake pedal travel is an indication that the rear brake-shoes require adjusting. The brakes on both rear wheels must be adjusted to regain even and efficient braking. Block the front wheels and jack up each rear wheel in turn. Fully release the hand brake. Turn the adjuster in a clockwise direction until the wheel is locked, then turn back until the wheel is free to rotate without the shoe rubbing. Adjust the other rear brake in a similar way. The hand brake is automatically adjusted at the same time. If, however, hand brake lever movement is excessive consult your Distributor/Dealer.

BRAKES

Preventive maintenance

In addition to the recommended periodical inspection of brake components it is advisable as the car ages and as a precaution against the effects of wear and deterioration, to make a more searching inspection and renew parts as necessary. It is recommended that:

(1) Disc brake pads, drum brake linings, hoses, and pipes should be examined at intervals no greater than those laid down in the Passport to Service.

(2) Brake fluid should be changed completely every 18 months or 24,000 miles (40000 km.) whichever is the sooner.

(3) All fluid seals in the hydraulic system and all flexible hoses should be examined and renewed if necessary every 3 years or 40,000 miles (65000 km.) whichever is the sooner. At the same time the working surface of the pistons and the bores of the master cylinder, wheel cylinders, and other slave cylinders should be examined and new parts fitted where necessary.

Care must be taken always to observe the following points:

(a) At all times use the recommended brake fluid.

(b) Never leave fluid in unsealed containers. It absorbs moisture quickly and this can be dangerous.

(c) Fluid drained from the system or used for bleeding is best discarded.

(d) The necessity for absolute cleanliness throughout cannot be over-emphasized.

STEERING AND SUSPENSION

Steering rack (early Tourer cars)

A lubricating nipple is provided on the steering pinion housing. The nipple is accessible from above on R.H.D. cars and from below the radiator on L.H.D. cars. To lubricate give not more than 10 strokes of an oil gun filled with oil to Ref. B (page 72).

Steering-column

The clamp bolts securing the universal joint to the steering-column must be checked periodically to ensure tightness. Do not overtighten.

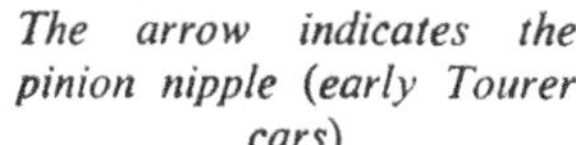

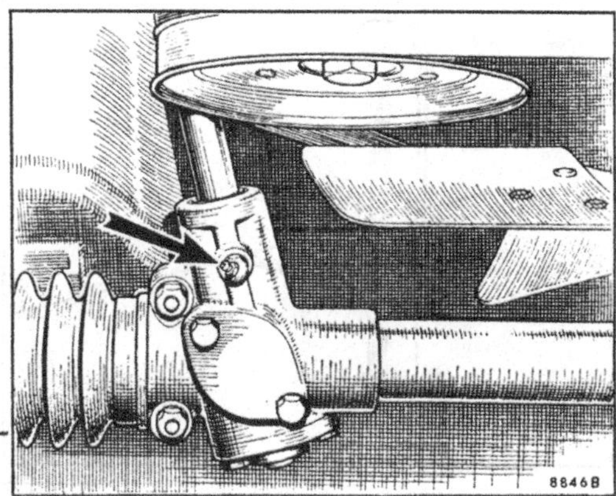

The arrow indicates the pinion nipple (early Tourer cars)

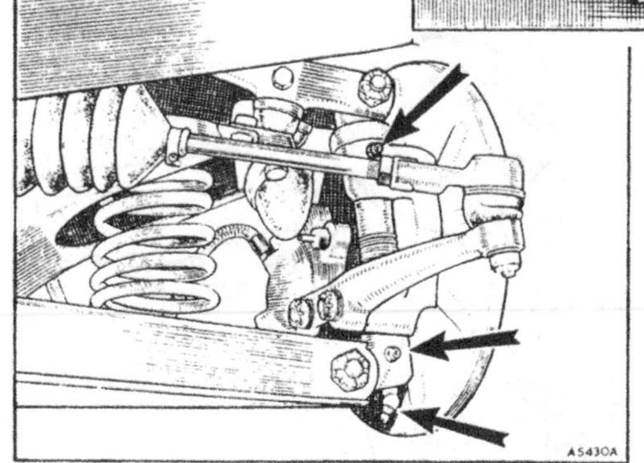

The front suspension lubrication nipples, which require regular attention. This illustration shows the left-hand side only

Front suspension

Lubrication nipples are provided on the top and bottom swivel pin bushes and in the base of each swivel pin; each nipple should be charged with grease.

Front wheel alignment

Excessive and uneven tyre wear is usually caused by faulty wheel alignment. The front wheels should be set with between $\frac{1}{16}$ and $\frac{3}{32}$ in. (1·5 and 2·3 mm.) toe-in, and care should be taken that the measurements are taken at axle level and that the rims run true.

Since correct alignment is so important and entails the use of a special gauge, this work should be entrusted to an authorized Distributor or Dealer.

WHEELS AND TYRES

Jacking up the car

The jack is designed to lift one side of the car at a time. Apply the hand brake, and if the car is on an incline it is advisable to scotch one of the wheels on the opposite side of the car to the one being jacked.

Insert the lifting arm of the jack into the socket. **Make certain that the jack lifting arm is pushed fully into the socket and that the base of the jack is on firm ground.** The jack should lean slightly outwards at the top to allow for the radial movement of the car as it is raised.

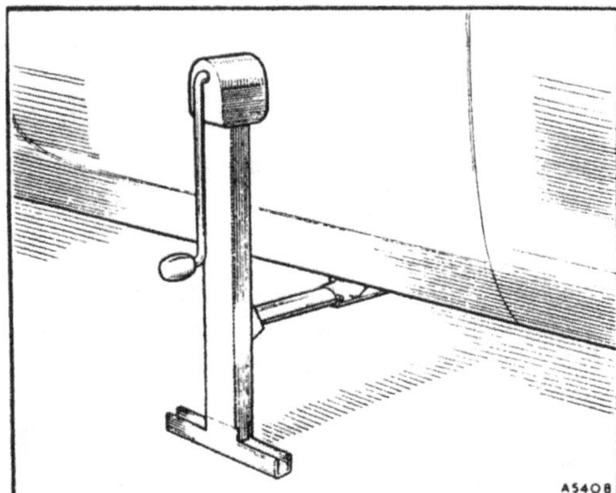

Jacking position

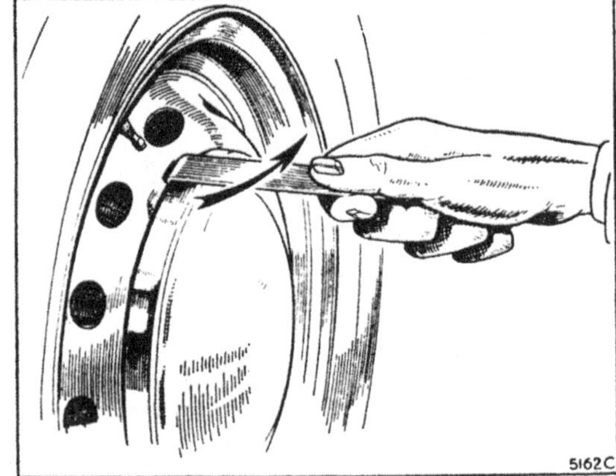

Removing a wheel disc

Jack maintenance

If the jack is neglected it may be difficult to use in a roadside emergency. Examine it occasionally, clean off accumulated dust, and lightly oil the thread to prevent the formation of rust.

Removing the wheel discs (pressed-steel wheels)

Insert the wheel disc lever in the recess provided in the road wheel and lever off the disc, using a sideways motion.

To refit the hub disc, place the rim over two of the buttons on the wheel centre and give the outer face a sharp blow with the hand over the third button.

Removing and replacing the wheels (pressed type)

Slacken the four nuts securing the road wheel to the hub; turn anti-clockwise to loosen and clockwise to tighten. Raise the car with the jack (page 56) to lift the wheel clear of the ground and remove the nuts. Withdraw the road wheel from the hub. When refitting the road wheel locate the wheel on the hub, lightly tighten the nuts with the wheel nut spanner (securing nuts must be fitted with the **taper side towards the wheel**), and lower the jack. Fully tighten the wheel nuts, tightening them diagonally and progressively, at the same time avoid overtightening.

Replace the hub cover.

Removing and replacing the wheels (wire type)

Use the mallet to slacken the winged hub nut or the spanner to slacken the octagonal hub nut used.

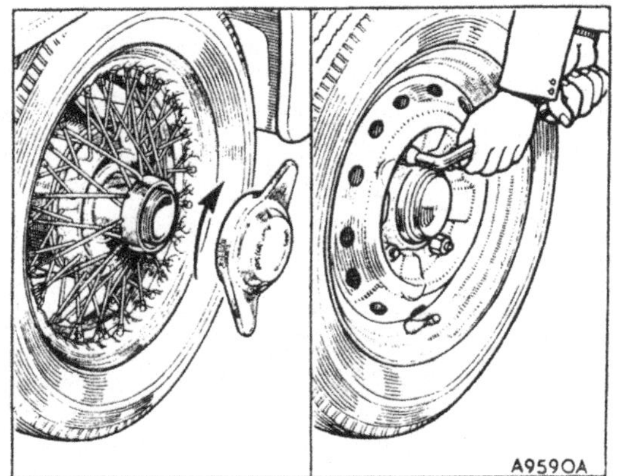

(Left) Turn the winged hub nuts clockwise to unscrew on the right-hand side of the car and anti-clockwise on the left-hand side

(Right) Removing the road wheel securing nuts (pressed type)

Care of wire wheels

(1) When the car is new, after the first long run or after 50 miles (80 km.) of short runs, jack up the wheels and hammer the nuts to make sure that they are tight.

(2) Always jack up a wheel before using the hammer, and always hammer the nuts tight.

(3) Locknuts are marked 'LEFT' or 'RIGHT' to show to which side of the car they must be fitted, and also with the word 'UNDO' and an arrow.

(4) Before replacing a wheel wipe all serrations, threads, and cones of the wheel and hub and then lightly coat them with grease. If a forced change is made on the road, remove, clean, and grease as soon as convenient.

(5) Once a year remove the wheels for examination and regreasing.

WHEELS AND TYRES

Tyre maintenance

To obtain the best tyre mileage and to suppress the development of irregular wear on the tyres the wheels can be interchanged diagonally bringing the spare wheel into use.

Excessive local distortion as a result of striking a kerb, a loose brick, a deep pot-hole, etc., may cause the casing cords to fracture.

Tyres, including the spare, must be maintained at the pressures recommended on page 5; check with an accurate tyre gauge at least once a week, and regulate as necessary. Pressures should be checked when the tyres are cold; do not reduce the pressure in warm tyres where the increase above the normal pressure is due to temperature.

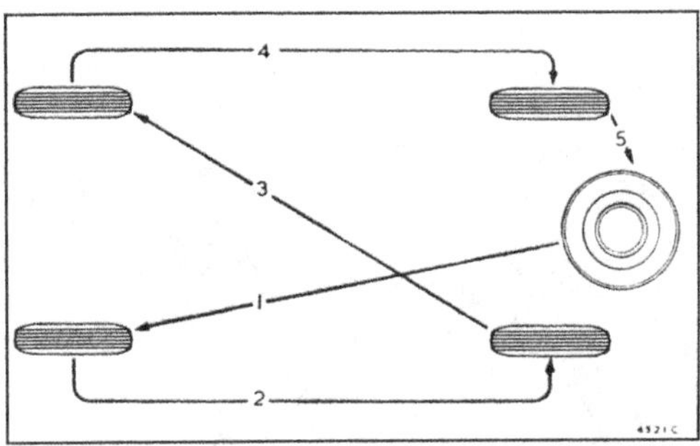

Two jacking operations only are required to interchange the road wheels in this order

See that the valve caps are screwed down firmly by hand. The cap prevents the entry of dirt into the valve mechanism and forms an additional seal on the valve, preventing any leakage if the valve core is damaged.

Flints and other sharp objects should be removed with a penknife or similar tool. If neglected, they may work through the cover.

Any oil or grease which may get onto the tyres should be cleaned off by using fuel sparingly. Do not use paraffin (kerosene), which has a detrimental effect on rubber.

When repairing tubes have punctures or injuries vulcanized. Ordinary patches should only be used for emergencies.

Vulcanizing is absolutely essential in the case of tubes manufactured from synthetic rubber.

Tyre replacement

Radial-ply (SP) tyres are optional equipment and if used they must be fitted in sets of four.

Tyre removal and refitting

Inextensible wires are incorporated in the edges of tyres. Do not attempt to stretch the edges of the tyre cover over the rim. Force is entirely unnecessary and dangerous, as it merely tends to damage the cover edges. Fitting or removing will be quite easy if the wire edges are carefully adjusted into the rim base. If the cover edge fits tightly on the rim seating it should be freed by using the tyre levers.

Remove all valve parts to deflate the tyre completely and push both cover

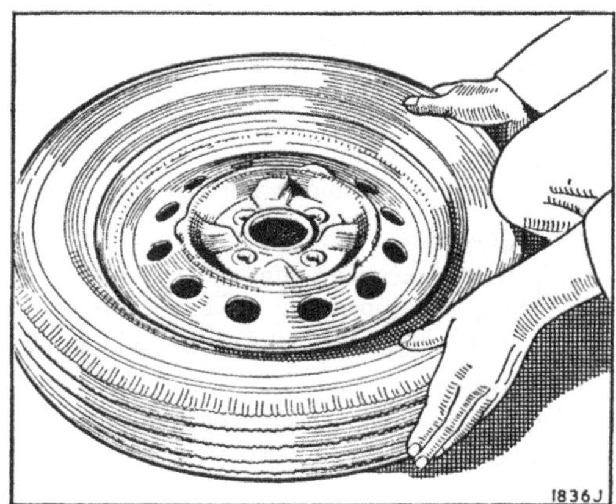

The cover beads should be pushed into the well-base of the rim opposite to the valve

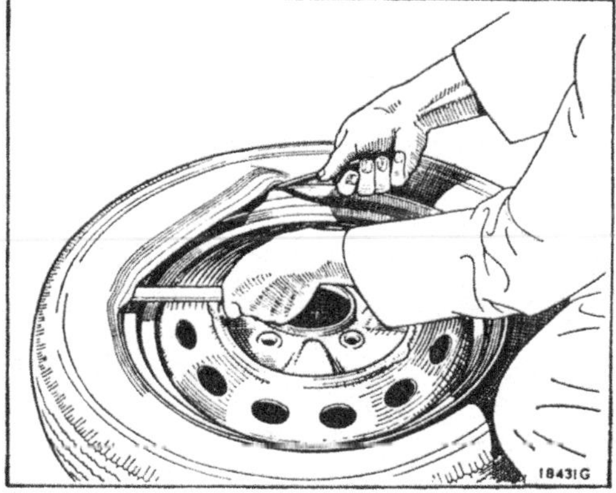

The cover edge can then be levered over the rim close to the valve position to remove it, or replace it, as required

edges into the base of the rim at the point diametrically opposite to the valve, then lever the cover edge near the valve over the rim edge (see illustration above).

This permits the tyre valve to be pushed through the hole in the rim and the inner tube to be withdrawn for attention when required.

A similar technique has to be employed when replacing the tyre, first fitting the tyre into the rim at a point opposite to the valve and finishing the fitting in the region of the valve, keeping the beaded edge in the well-base of the rim.

MAINTENANCE SUMMARY

Weekly

Inspect engine oil level, and top up as necessary.
Check water level in radiator, and top up if necessary.
Check battery and top up to correct levels.
Test tyre pressures.

3,000 miles (5000 km.) or 3 months service

1. *Engine*
   Top up carburetter piston dampers.
   Check the coolant level in radiator.
   Top up windscreen washer bottle.

2. *Clutch*
   Check level of fluid in the hydraulic clutch master cylinder.

3. *Brakes*
   Check brakes, and adjust if necessary.
   Make visual inspection of brake lines and pipes.
   Check level of fluid in the hydraulic brake master cylinder.

4. *Electrical*
   Check batteries, and top up to correct level.
   Check headlamp alignment.

5. *Lubrication*
   Check and top up engine oil level.
   Change engine oil (if using monograde only).
   Lubricate all grease nipples (except steering rack and pinion).

6. *Wheels and tyres*
   Check tyre pressures.

6,000 miles (10000 km.) or 6 months service

1. *Engine*
   Top up carburetter piston dampers.
   Check fan belt tension.
   Check valve rocker clearances, and adjust if necessary.
   Check the coolant level in radiator.
   Top up windscreen washer bottle.

2. *Ignition*
   Check automatic retard and advance mechanism.
   Check distributor contact points, and adjust if necessary.
   Lubricate all distributor parts as necessary.
   Clean and adjust sparking plugs.

3. *Clutch*
   Check level of fluid in the hydraulic clutch master cylinder.

4. *Steering*
   Check wheel alignment, and adjust if necessary.

5. *Brakes*
   Check brakes, and adjust if necessary.
   Make visual inspection of brake lines and pipes.
   Check level of fluid in the hydraulic brake master cylinder.
   Inspect the disc brake friction pads and report if attention is required.

6. *Electrical*
   Check battery cell specific gravity readings and top up to correct level.
   Check all lamps for correct functioning.
   Check headlamp alignment.

7. *Lubrication*
   Change oil in engine.
   Lubricate dynamo end bearing.
   Top up gearbox, overdrive (if applicable), and rear axle oil levels.
   Fit new oil filter element.
   Lubricate all grease nipples (except steering rack and pinion).
   Lubricate door locks and hinges.
   Clean overdrive filter element.

8. *Wheels and tyres*
   Check tyre pressures.

9,000 miles (15000 km.) or 9 months service

Carry out the **3,000 miles (5000 km.) or 3 months service.**

12,000 miles (20000 km.) or 12 months service

1. *Engine*
   Top up carburetter piston dampers.
   Renew air filter elements.
   Check valve rocker clearances, and adjust if necessary.
   Check fan belt tension.
   Lubricate water pump sparingly.
   Check coolant level in radiator, and top up if necessary.
   Top up windscreen washer bottle.
   Crankcase closed-circuit breathing system; change engine oil filler cap and
      clean crankcase breather valve.

2. *Ignition*
   Check automatic retard and advance mechanism.
   Clean, and adjust distributor contact points.
   Lubricate all distributor parts as necessary.
   Fit new sparking plugs.

3. *Clutch*
   Check level of fluid in the hydraulic clutch master cylinder.

MAINTENANCE SUMMARY

4. *Steering*
   Check steering and suspension moving parts for wear.
   Check wheel alignment, and adjust if necessary.
   Check steering column-pinch bolts for tightness.

5. *Brakes*
   Check brakes, and adjust if necessary.
   Make visual inspection of brake lines and pipes.
   Check level of fluid in the hydraulic brake master cylinder.
   Inspect disc brake friction pads and report if attention is required.
   Inspect and blow out brake linings and drums.

6. *General*
   Tighten rear road spring seat bolts.

7. *Electrical*
   Check battery cell specific gravity readings and top up to correct level.
   Check all lamps for correct functioning.
   Check headlamp alignment.

8. *Lubrication*
   Change oil in engine.
   Lubricate dynamo bearing.
   Top up gearbox, overdrive (if applicable), and rear axle oil levels.
   Fit new oil filter element.
   Lubricate steering rack and pinion.
   Lubricate steering rack and pinion (early Tourer cars).
   Lubricate all grease nipples.
   Clean overdrive filter element.

9. *Wheels and tyres*
   Check tyre pressures.

NOTE. Take the advice of your Distributor/Dealer on:
   1. The need for more frequent engine oil changes.
   2. When to change round road wheels.
   3. When to check and adjust headlight beams.

THE BMC SERVICE FACTORY EXCHANGE UNIT SCHEME

The BMC Service Factory Exchange Unit Scheme

The BMC Exchange Scheme—the most comprehensive in Europe—has been designed specifically to **save you money.**

Briefly, the scheme covers practically every major assembly on any BMC car marketed in the last 10 years, and includes components such as heaters and servo units for brakes as well as a wide range of instruments.

If, for example, you want another engine, the Distributor returns the old one to us, and we issue one which has been fully reconditioned in one of our own specialist factories.

By using this technique the cost is considerably reduced but **not the quality,** and each replacement unit carries the same factory warranty as a brand-new one.

Your BMC Distributor or Dealer will be pleased to give you full details and comparative examples of the money which you can save by taking advantage of this scheme.

Units available

Engines and Ancillaries

Clutches

Gearboxes

Rear Axles and Differential Assemblies

Braking System Units

Steering Gears

Instruments

Electrical Units

Bumper Bars

Fuel Pumps

Shock Absorbers

Heaters

SUPPLEMENTARY TOOL KIT

To supplement the tool kit a waterproof canvas roll containing the following is obtainable from all Distributors. Part number AKF 1596 should be quoted.

6 spanners:
$\frac{5}{16}$ in. × $\frac{3}{8}$ in. A.F.
$\frac{7}{16}$ in. × $\frac{1}{2}$ in. A.F.
$\frac{1}{2}$ in. × $\frac{9}{16}$ in. A.F.
$\frac{9}{16}$ in. × $\frac{5}{8}$ in. A.F.
$\frac{11}{16}$ in. × $\frac{13}{16}$ in. A.F.
$\frac{3}{4}$ in. × $\frac{7}{8}$ in. A.F.

1 pair 6 in. pliers.

1 7 in. × $\frac{3}{8}$ in. diameter tommy-bar.

1 $\frac{1}{2}$ in. × $\frac{9}{16}$ in. A.F. tubular spanner.

2 screwdrivers.

INDEX

LUBRICATION CHART

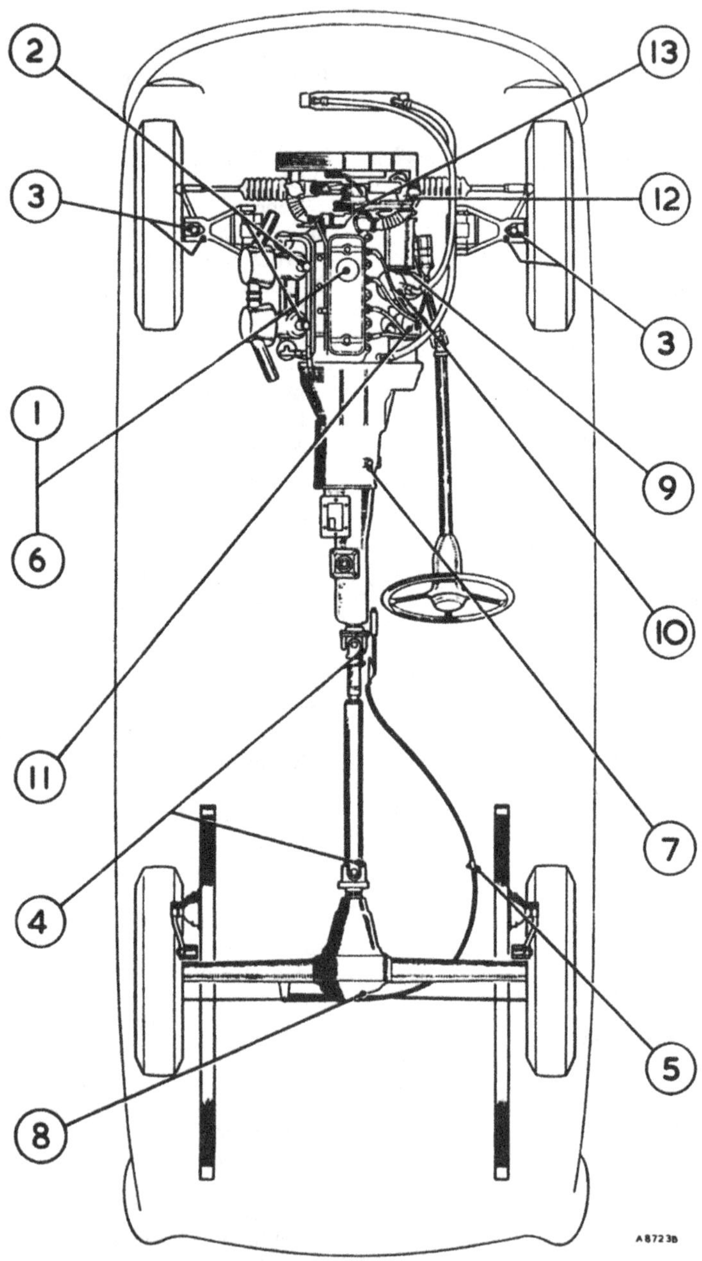

KEY TO LUBRICATION CHART

Weekly

(1) ENGINE. Check oil level with the dipstick, and replenish if necessary with new oil to **Ref. A**.

Every 3,000 miles (5000 km.) or 3 months

(2) CARBURETTERS. Remove the cap from each suction chamber and insert a small quantity of oil to Ref. E. Lubricate the carburetter controls.

(3) FRONT SUSPENSION. Charge each upper and lower swivel pin bush and the lower swivel pin nipple with grease to Ref. C.

(4) PROPELLER SHAFT. Charge each universal joint nipple (early Tourer cars) and sliding yoke nipple with grease to Ref. C.

(5) HAND BRAKE CABLE Charge the nipple on the hand brake cable with grease to Ref. C.

Every 6,000 miles (10000 km.) or 6 months

(6) ENGINE. Drain the used oil from the sump and refill to the 'MAX' mark on the dipstick with new oil to Ref. A.

(7) GEARBOX AND OVER-DRIVE. Check the oil level with the dipstick, and replenish if necessary with new oil to Ref. A.

(8) REAR AXLE. Replenish if necessary to the level of the filler plug with new oil to **Ref. B**.

(9) DYNAMO. Add two drops of oil to Ref. E to the hole in the rear end bearing plate.

(10) OIL FILTER. Renew the element and wash the bowl in fuel.

(11) DISTRIBUTOR. Withdraw rotating arm and add a few drops of oil to Ref. E to opening and also to advance mechanism through gap around cam spindle. Smear cam and pivot pin with grease or oil.

Every 12,000 miles (20000 km.) or 12 months

(12) STEERING. (Early Tourer cars.) Apply an oilgun containing oil to Ref. B to the nipple and give several strokes.

(13) WATER PUMP. Remove the plug on the body and add a small quantity of grease to Ref. C.

NOTES.—Oil and grease references are detailed on page 70.

The engine oil change periods are those recommended when a multigrade oil is used. Monograde or single viscosity oil should be changed at 3,000 mile (5000 km.) or 3 month intervals.

KEY TO RECOMMENDED LUBRICANTS

	A			B		C	D	E
	Engine and Gearbox			Rear Axle and Steering Gear		All Grease Points	Upper Cylinder Lubricant	Oilcan and Carburetter
Component	Tropical and temperate down to 5° C. (41° F.)	Extreme cold temperatures between 5° C. (41° F.) and −12° C. (10° F.)	Arctic conditions temperatures consistently below −12° C. (10° F.)	All conditions down to −12° C. (10° F.)	Arctic consistently below −12° C. (10° F.)			
Climatic conditions predominating						All conditions	All conditions	All conditions
MOBIL	Mobil Special 20W/40 Mobil A.F.	Mobil Arctic or Mobiloil Special 10W/30 or 10W/40	Mobiloil Special 10W/30 Mobiloil 10W Mobiloil Super 10W/40	Mobilube G.X. 90	Mobilube G.X. 80	Mobilgrease M.P.	Mobil Upperlube	Mobiloil Special 10W/30 Mobiloil Super 10W/40
ESSO	Esso Motor Oil 40/50 Esso Motor Oil 40 Esso Extra Motor Oil 20/40	Esso Motor Oil 20 or 20W/30 Esso Extra Motor Oil 10W/30	Esso Motor Oil 10W Esso Extra Motor Oil	Esso Gear Oil G.P. 90/40 or G.P. 90	Esso Gear Oil G.P.80	Esso Multi-purpose Grease H	Esso Upper Cylinder Lubricant	Esso Extra Motor Oil 10W/30
FILTRATE	Filtrate Heavy Filtrate 20W/50	Filtrate Zero or Filtrate 10W/30	Filtrate Sub-Zero 10W or Filtrate 10W/30	Filtrate E.P. Grease 90	Filtrate E.P. Gear 80	Filtrate Super Lithium Grease	Filtrate Petroyle	Filtrate 10W/30 Multigrade
BP	Energol S.A.E. 40 or Super Visco-Static 20W/50	Energol S.A.E. 20W Super Visco-Static 10W/40 or Visco-Static	Energol S.A.E. 10W Super Visco-Static 10W/40 or Visco-Static	BP Gear Oil S.A.E. 90 E.P.	BP Gear Oil S.A.E. 80 E.P.	Energrease L. 2	BP Upper Cylinder Lubricant	Visco-Static or Super Visco-Static 10W/40
SHELL	Shell Super Motor Oil Shell X—100 40 Shell X—100 Multigrade 20W/40 or 20W/50	Shell Super Motor Oil Shell X—100 20W Shell X—100 Multigrade 10W/30 or 20W/40, or 20W/50	Shell Super Motor Oil or Shell X—100 10W Shell X—100 Multigrade 10W/30	Spirax 90 E.P.	Spirax 80 E.P.	Shell Retinax A	Shell Upper Cylinder Lubricant	Shell Super Motor Oil
CASTROL	Castrol X.L.	Castrolite or Castrol X.L.	Castrol Z or Castrolite	Castrol Hypoy	Castrol Hypoy Light	Castrolease L.H.	Castrollo	Castrolite
DUCKHAM'S	Q. 20/50	Q. 20/50 or Q. 5500	Q. 5500	Duckham's Hypoid 90	Duckham's Hypoid 90	Duckham's L.B.10 Grease	Duckham's Adcoid Liquid	Q. 5500
STERNOL	Sternol W.W. 40 or W.W. Multigrade 20W/50	Sternol W.W. 20 or W.W. Multigrade 10W/40 or 20W/50	Sternol W.W. 10 or W.W. Multigrade 10W/40	Ambroleum E.P. 90	Ambroleum E.P. 80	Ambroline L.H.T.	Sternol Magikoyl	Sternol W.W. Multigrade 10W/40

Brooklands Books Ltd., PO Box 904, Amersham, Bucks. UK

brooklandsboooks.com

Part Number: AKD 3900 J

ISBN: 9781855200609   Ref: MG74HH   2336/9W5

OFFICIAL TECHNICAL BOOKS

Brooklands Technical Books has been formed to supply owners, restorers and professional repairers with official factory literature.

Workshop Manuals

Midget Instruction Manual		9781855200739
Midget TD & TF	AKD580A	9781870642552
MGA 1500 1600 & 1600 Mk. 2	AKD600D	9781869826307
MGA Twin Cam	AKD926B	9781855208179
Austin-Healey Sprite Mk. 2, Mk. 3 & Mk. 4 and		
MG Midget Mk. 1, Mk. 2 & Mk. 3		
	AKD4021	9781855202818
Midget 1500	AKM4071B	9781855201699
MGB & MGB GT	AKD3259 & AKD4957	9781855201743
MGB GT V8 Supplement		9781855201859
MGB, MGB GT and MGB GT V8		9781783180578
MGC	AKD 7133	9781855201828
Rover 25 & MG ZR 1999-2005		
	RCL0534ENGBB	9781855208834
Rover 75 & MG ZT 1999-2005		
	RCL0536ENGBB	9781855208841
MGF - 1.6 MPi, 1.8 MPi, 1.8VVC		
RCL 0051ENG, RCL0057ENG		
	& RCL0124	9781855207165
MGF Electrical Manual 1996-2000 MY		
	RCL0341	9781855209077
MG TF	RCL0493	9781855207493

Parts Catalogues

MGA 1500	AKD1055	9781870642569
MGA 1600 Mk. 1 & Mk. 2	AKD1215	9781870642613
Austin-Healey Sprite Mk. 1 & Mk. 2 and		
MG Midget Mk. 1 (Mechanical & Body Edition)		
	AKD3566 & AKD3567	9781783180509
Austin-Healey Sprite Mk. 3 & Mk. 4 and		
MG Midget Mk. 2 & Mk. 3 (Mechanical & Body		
Edition 1969)	AKD3513 & AKD3514	9781783180554
Austin-Healey Sprite Mk. 3 & Mk. 4 and		
MG Midget Mk. 2 & Mk. 3 (Feb 1977 Edition)		
	AKM0036	9780948207419
MGB up to Sept 1976	AKM0039	9780948207068
MGB Sept 1976 on	AKM0037	9780948207440

Owners Handbooks

Midget Series TD		9781870642910
Midget TF and TF 1500		
Operation Manual	AKD658A	9781870642934
MGA 1500	AKD598G	9781855202924
MGA 1600	AKD1172C	9781855201668
MGA 1600 Mk. 2	AKD1958A	9781855201675
MGA Twin Cam (Operation)	AKD879	9781855207929
MGA Twin Cam (Operation)	AKD879B	9781855207936
MGA 1500 Special Tuning	AKD819A	9781783181728
MGA 1500 and 1600 Mk. 1 Special Tuning		
	AKD819B	9781783181735
Midget TF and TF 1500	AKD210A	9781855202979
Midget Mk. 3 (GB 1967-74)	AKD7596	9781855201477
Midget (Pub 1978)	AKM3229	9781855200906
Midget Mk. 3 (US 1967-74)	AKD7883	9781855206311
Midget Mk. 3 (US 1976)	AKM3436	9781855201767
Midget Mk. 3 (US 1979)	AKM4386	9781855201774
MGB Tourer (Pub 1965)	AKD3900C	9781869826741

MGB Tourer & GT (Pub 1969)	AKD3900J	9781855200609
MGB Tourer & GT (Pub 1974)	AKD7598	9781869826727
MGB Tourer & GT (Pub 1976)	AKM3661	9781869826703
MGB GT V8	AKD8423	9781869826710
MGB Tourer & GT (US 1968)	AKD7059B	9781870642514
MGB Tourer & GT (US 1971)	AKD7881	9781870642521
MGB Tourer & GT (US 1973)	AKD8155	9781870642538
MGB Tourer (US 1975)	AKD3286	9781870642545
MGB (US 1979)	AKM8098	9781855200722
MGB Tourer & GT Tuning	CAKD4034L	9780948207051
MGB Special Tuning 1800cc	AKD4034	9780948207006
MGC	AKD4887B	9781869826734
MGF (Modern shape)	RCL0332ENG	9781855208339

Owners Workshop Manuals - Autobooks

MGA & MGB & GT 1955-1968	
(Glove Box Autobooks Manual)	9781855200937
MGA & MGB & GT 1955-1968	
(Autobooks Manual)	9781783180356
Austin-Healey Sprite Mk. 1, 2, 3 & 4 and	
MG Midget Mk. 1, 2, 3 & 1500 1958-1980	
(Glove Box Autobooks Manual)	9781855201255
Austin-Healey Sprite Mk. 1, 2, 3 & 4 and	
MG Midget Mk. 1, 2, 3 & 1500 1958-1980	
(Autobooks Manual)	9781783180332
MGB & MGB GT 1968-1981	
(Glove Box Autobooks Manual)	9781855200944
MGB & MGB GT 1968-1981	
(Autobooks Manual)	9781783180325

Carburetters

SU Carburetters Tuning Tips & Techniques	
	9781855202559
Solex Carburetters Tuning Tips & Techniques	
	9781855209770
Weber Carburettors Tuning Tips and Techniques	
	9781855207592

Restoration Guide

MG T Series Restoration Guide	9781855202115
MGA Restoration Guide	9781855203020
Restoring Sprites & Midgets	9781855205987
Practical Classics On MGB Restoration	9780946489428

MG - Road Test Books

MG Gold Portfolio 1929-1939	9781855201941
MG TA & TC GOLD PORT 1936-1949	9781855203150
MG TD & TF Gold Portfolio 1949-1955	9781855203167
MG Y-Type & Magnette Road Test Portfolio	9781855208629
MGB & MGC GT V8 GP 1962-1980	9781855200715
MGA & Twin Cam Gold Portfolio 1955-1962	9781855200784
MGB Roadsters 1962-1980	9781869826109
MGC & MGB GT V8 LEX	9781855203631
MG Midget Road Test Portfolio 1961-1979	9781855208957
MGF & TF Performance Portfolio 1995-2005	9781855207073
Road & Track On MG Cars 1949-1961	9780946489398
Road & Track On MG Cars 1962-1980	9780946489817

Brooklands Books Ltd., P.O. Box 904, Amersham, Bucks, HP6 9JA, England, UK

www.brooklandsbooks.com

Made in the USA
Monee, IL
07 July 2026

56552037R00046